The Nature of Belief

General editors of this book and others in the *Issues in Relgious Studies* series: Peter Baelz and Jean Holm

The Nature of Belief

Elizabeth Maclaren

HAWTHORN BOOKS, INC.
Publishers/NEW YORK

First published in Great Britain in 1976 by Sheldon Press, Marylebone Road, London NW1 4DU.

First published in the United States in 1976 by Hawthorn Books, Inc., 260 Madison Avenue, New York, New York 10016.

'I will not hammer the walls too close.
I shall leave plenty of silences.'
                    IAN CRICHTON SMITH

FOR
G.M.G.
my first theological mentor

ELIZABETH MACLAREN was born and brought up in Glasgow where she took a master's degree in English Literature and Philosophy. She then read for a degree in Systematic Theology at Edinburgh University. Her interest in the Christian-Marxist interaction has taken her on several visits to Czechoslovakia. She now lives in Edinburgh and lectures in the Department of Divinity in the University of Edinburgh.

CONTENTS

PREFACE

As soon as people begin to discuss anything in religion, they are liable to disagree. Does God exist? Can non-Christians be saved? Is it possible that men will be recognizably alive after death? Was Jesus able to want anything God didn't want?

Once the discussion progresses a little, it emerges that the arguments in the foreground are not the whole story. One person expects to persuade another to change his mind by rational argument. Someone else is convinced that only direct intervention by God can teach anyone the truth on religious issues. One holds everyone responsible for his own beliefs. Another finds everyone determined by factors outside his will.

Often these 'second-order' differences are more basic than the immediate ones with which the conversation began. They lie below the surface of every specific question that comes up, and often affect our whole attitude and approach.

For that reason it helps to examine them, to bring them out of the background a little, and see what comes of holding them up to the light. That is what this exploration of 'the nature of belief' hopes to provoke. I cannot say that studying the various questions the book raises will lead to an 'official solution'. Probably on such matters official solutions are impossible and dangerous. All I hope is that facing these questions will clarify people's stances on belief, at least to themselves.

My thanks for help and encouragement with the text to Professor Peter Baelz and Miss Jean Holm; and for typing assistance to Miss Elma Webster, Mrs M. Robertson and my father.

The Nature of Belief

1

THE NATURE OF BELIEF

'I can't believe *that!*' said Alice.
'Can't you?' the Queen said in a pitying tone. 'Try again:
draw a long breath and shut your eyes.'
Alice laughed. 'There's no use trying,' she said: 'one *can't*
believe impossible things.'
'I daresay you haven't had much practice,' said the Queen.
'When I was your age I always did it for half-an-hour a day.
Why, sometimes I've believed as many as six impossible
things before breakfast.'
LEWIS CARROLL   Through the Looking-Glass

To many alert and sensitive people today, 'having religious faith'
means believing impossible things without the time limit set
by breakfast. In a world lacerated by pain and cruelty, how can
the existence of a loving God be affirmed? What does it mean
to claim that the cynical, weary, exploitative world has been
saved? How can men maintain that Jesus is lord of history
as churches empty and institutions creak?

Not only sceptics may find it incredible. In some moods at
least, the believer must ask *himself* how on earth he believes. He
too meets people dying of cancer and watches television news
bulletins. He rubs shoulders, more than the unbeliever, with
the unloveliness of ecclesiastical life. Every so often his Sunday
paper comes up with conclusive arguments that Jesus was a
sacred mushroom, or that his bones have been dug up in
Palestine. At a more sophisticated level, he may be aware of the
problems of identifying the actual words and deeds of the historical Jesus. If he has understood enough philosophy to destroy
his instilled modesty before words like 'God', 'mystery', 'infinite',
he may be nagged by worry about whether they mean anything
at all. As a post-Freudian, he must wonder if he only believes
because of emotional needs. As a man of the world, he must

1

ask if he's a Christian only because he grew up in Britain and not in Bengal.

How, in such complexity, is belief possible?

The range of answers to that question will vary widely, depending on the stance of the answerer. 'It's possible because people are indoctrinated in their youth, and never learn to think critically.' 'It's possible by the grace of God.' 'It's just that some temperaments need to feel that kind of security.' 'Well, everyone needs to believe in something, don't they?' 'You find the strength to go on believing if you have faith.'

Some people already know where they stand on the matter. They believe or disbelieve confidently, and are rarely moved to consider any alternative position. Others find it more difficult, see something to be said for most of the arguments, but nothing conclusive for any, and oscillate between belief and unbelief. In so far as this book has a stance, it is nearer the latter position than the former. It will not *settle* the question of the nature of belief, but it will try to explore it as open-mindedly as possible.

Of course, even open-mindedness may be dangerous. When does it become fence-sitting, an uncommendable refusal to take a stand? Should one, for example, go on being open-minded about apartheid, or about anarchism, or about totally unrestricted freedom of speech? Somewhere in the course of the discussion, we shall have to consider the charge that agnosticism about Christian belief is some kind of failure. It would, however, be an over-simplification to *assume* anything of the sort as a starting point.

Why, then, is it a complex issue?

Initially we are concerning ourselves mainly with Christian belief. That might seem to make matters simple, since we don't then have to deal with all the range of human belief, but with only one segment of it. But, even here, perplexities abound. 'Belief', in English, can mean two things: (1) the content, what is believed; and (2) the believing, the attitude, disposition, mental state involved in holding the belief. Neither of these refers to an obvious identifiable thing.

Suppose we consider first the substantial sense of belief, that which is believed. How is this settled for Christianity? What *is* Christian belief? To begin with it might seem obvious: something like the creeds, the Bible, belief in Jesus, belonging to the

2

church, following a certain ethical code. But when you scan the history of Christendom, one man's belief is fairly often another man's anathema. While fourth-century Christians would have died or shed blood over every vowel of the Creeds, sixteenth-century Christians were denouncing them as human fabrications. While many Roman Catholics commit themselves to the authority of the Papacy, many militant Protestants denounce the Pope as Antichrist. Some who claim to believe the Bible understand this to involve literal adherence to every indicative sentence, literal obedience to every command. Others who make the same claim find it possible to accept such generous interpretation that they actually hold beliefs directly opposed to those of their fellow-Biblicists.

Arguments about who counts as 'the Church' are legion. Followers of Jesus who express their faith in terms of a human/divine figure rage against the 'crypto-humanists' who concentrate only on the human, historical man. The same 'humanists' accuse the theologians of Christological mystification. Even when men say the same words, a little probing frequently exposes the fact that they mean them quite differently. (I once asked thirteen students to paraphrase as accurately as they could the sentence 'God exists', and was given nine substantially distinct answers.)

Furthermore, even if theoretical agreement is reached about dogma, people worship very differently and live in radically opposed ways. Do they all then believe the same thing or not? Does Christian belief *necessarily* involve a practical component in its reference, or can it be defined independently of life style and liturgy?

This mass of complications is the tip of an iceberg obvious even to fairly casual pleasure boats on the theological sea. Underwater explorers can chart an immense bulk of submerged matter, which is the main professional concern of theologians, and actually inseparable from the surface questions. Even the visible tip, however, is enough to show the difficulty of initially identifying Christian belief.

This obviously affects the question of how belief is possible. On some understandings of belief, for instance that Christian belief means following Jesus' ethic—(did Jesus have an ethic?)—consistent practice might be hard to achieve, but intentional assent relatively easy. On the other hand, if belief is taken to

3

mean acceptance of all the dogmas of some statement of belief, even theoretical agreement might be really baffling. Many accounts of what it means to believe make things easier for themselves by begging the question of what it *is* that must be believed. We must try to keep all the balls in the air for a little longer.

There are some kinds of disagreement where the issue can be settled quite easily, in principle at least. If you tell me you believe that John has come back from his holiday and I say I don't believe it, it's easy to find out which is right. We ring his doorbell, or 'phone, or check if his milk and newspapers are being delivered. Except in the most unusual circumstances of his lying low and obliterating all traces of his return, a limited amount of patient attention would decide the matter.

Again, one might be involved in a dispute about the future, say about whether the Labour Party might be expected to win the next General Election by a substantial majority. One might not be able to decide conclusively on this one, even with the help of opinion polls, statistics, projections and hunches. Still, the question would be conclusively settled as soon as the Election took place.

On the other hand, suppose you're arguing about whether Keats is a greater poet than Shelley. Things are more difficult here. You know, of course, what your own instinctive preference is, but if you have any training in literary criticism this may not settle the question (though if you have a great deal of training in critical appreciation it may! Skilled critics can sometimes trust their sixth sense before they can explain it.) You might then consider elements in both which deserve notice, the richness of Keats' imagery, the intellectual energy of Shelley. You might debate whether Keats isn't a little too lush at times, or Shelley too uncompromisingly abstract. In the course of the discussion you might find you disagreed about what mattered most in a poet anyway. One might count ideas more important than expression (assuming such a distinction exists), the other might think rhythm more important than imagery. That is, in addition to discussing the merits and demerits of Keats and Shelley, you would be disputing the criteria of greatness in a poet. At both levels there might still be deadlock.

You might then decide to take past critical consensus into

4

the reckoning. But no critical consensus emerges. Some of the critics whom you mutually regard as trustworthy rate Keats higher than Shelley. Others make the reverse judgement. They too disagree both on specific points of poetic merit and on general criteria of excellence. No further appeal to critical authority will settle the question finally. What else is there to do? In the end you may agree to differ, or become literary enemies over the issue. With luck, you may go on reading both with constant attention, trying to be as open as possible to the poetic virtues or defects of both. Or you may abandon the whole question as pointless and a waste of time.

'The question of religious belief' is in a somewhat similar way not one but many questions. Some are historical or scientific, dealing with relatively straightforward facts. Some are philosophical, demanding a scrutiny of key religious concepts. Some are psychological, some are ethical, some are doctrinal. The more interesting ones shift from being of the simple factual type described above, to being more subtle and evaluative, like the aesthetic debate about Keats and Shelley.

So much, for the moment, for the substance of belief, the allegedly distinctive and distinguishing content of the Christian Faith. As if that did not present enough complexity, there is a further barrage of questions about the nature and status of believing whatever is believed. Can religious belief be classed as a subsection of belief in general, like political belief or economic belief, or is it something entirely different? Is religious belief properly to be understood in a quite distinct category, as *sui generis*? Do all examples of believing have something in common, or how is the concept of believing distinguished from such others as seeing, knowing, judging?

There is a sharp divide of opinion here between those who assume that examples of what it is to believe in other spheres are relevant to religious belief, and those who deny it. The latter have often been theologians, suggesting that faith is a special gift of God, totally unlike other beliefs which must be understood quite differently as merely human convictions.

It would obviously be unfair at the outset of such a book as this to *assume* one position or the other. As a matter of method, I shall begin by talking as if there was enough in common between religious belief and any other kind for it to be worth

5

making comparisons. Since I am well aware of a large body of opinion (mainly Protestant) who would regard this as building upon sand, I promise that the counter-position will not be suppressed. But if such a conclusion turns out to be reached, it is so strongly uncommonsensical that it has to be *seen* to be reached.

About believing in general we have again a heap of questions, among them the question whether there *is* such a thing as believing in general. Let us return at this point to the White Queen's conversation with Alice. It's funny, of course, but *why* is it funny? There is some kind of tension between the surface of the conversation and the substance of it which makes it into nonsense. This becomes clearer if one substitutes another verb for 'believe'. Suppose, for example, that the Queen has asked Alice to sing an incredibly difficult piece of modern music.

'I can't sing *that*!' said Alice.
'Can't you?' the Queen said in a pitying tone. 'Try again, draw a long breath, and shut your eyes.'
Alice laughed. 'There's no use trying,' she said: 'one *can't* sing impossible things.'
'I daresay you haven't had much practice,' said the Queen. 'When I was your age I always did it for half-an-hour a day. Why, sometimes I've sung as many as six impossible things before breakfast.'

This substitution almost destroys the comic absurdity of the original passage. If the song were *really* impossible, not even the White Queen could have sung it. In idiomatic English, however, it's possible enough, as a way of being emphatic, to say, 'I climbed an impossible mountain' or 'I've just finished knitting an impossible pattern'. 'Impossible' in such cases indicated something incredibly difficult, as in the proud boast of the agency who claimed, 'The difficult we can do at once. The impossible takes a little longer.' In that sense, even 'believing the impossible' might be intelligible: 'I think John's going to propose to Mary. I saw him come out of the jeweller's shop looking very self-conscious.' 'Never! I'm sure he's got no intention of marrying her. It's impossible.' 'I know it's impossible but I do believe it!'

The rich nonsense of the Alice conversation however doesn't

really depend on the play between literal and idiomatic senses of 'doing the impossible'. Rather it has to do with the fact that the subject of the conversation is *belief*. The words she chooses, 'try', 'practice', 'for half-an-hour a day' all suggest something you can do for a limited period and then stop, something that improves the more you do of it, and for the doing of which there are recognizable techniques.

All this is ludicrous when applied to belief. You may be able to remember when you first came to believe something or other, but normally the believing doesn't have an exact duration, certainly not in hours. Or if you can measure exactly ('I believed for half-an-hour that he'd been drowned until we had a message to say he's been picked up safely'), you can't normally believe repeatedly 'for half-an-hour *a day*'.[1] In retrospect people may remember an episode or episodes of belief, say in the Communist Party, or in Christianity, but such oscillation is not usually deliberate, nor, at the time, something one can start and stop at will.

Indeed, one of the main questions raised by the subject of belief is whether one can *ever* believe things by trying. How many of my beliefs do I ever decide on? How many do I just find myself believing? Is my belief about anything related to my will, or volition? What on earth could it mean to try to believe? Let alone impossible things, isn't it odd enough to talk of trying to believe *possible* things. What kind of procedure would it be to try to believe something? Would shutting your eyes and taking a long breath help?

Similar difficulties arise with the notion of practising a belief, especially of practising it for a certain length of time. Of course we can strain to imagine contexts which might make sense of such talk. We can think of someone concentrating very hard on what he believes, keeping it at the forefront of his mind, not letting himself forget it. But it's hardly natural to call even that practising belief. People often speak of 'practising Christians' and Brother Lawrence wrote on 'The Practice of the

---

[1] It has subsequently been pointed out to me by a sixth former that it is quite possible to wake up day after day believing for half-an-hour that life isn't worth living, and then changing one's mind. While being indebted for the observation, I find it leaves intact my conviction that such belief is not being *adopted* for a specified, chosen time.

Presence of God', but while the belief in such cases is being *put into practice*, it is less convincing to say that such people are *practising believing*. Suppose an agnostic went to church every so often, and said to himself at the church door: 'Now just you imagine for the next hour that you're a Christian, and imagine what it would be like to believe all that.' And suppose he managed to achieve a 'willing suspension of disbelief'. We would still hesitate to say he was *really* believing. Though someone practising playing the piano is *really* playing it.

The oddity of the Lewis Carroll passage takes us into many of the major philosophical issues about belief which must be touched on during this discussion. They cannot, within the scope of this book, be treated with the detail and historical reference that a more advanced work would demand. The reading lists, however, show something of the scope of the discussion.

The specific objective of this exercise is to forge links between some aspects of the question of belief which are usually handled more thoroughly, but in isolation. Philosophers, for example, often discuss the logical limits of what can sensibly be said or thought, as if these were fixed and absolute. Sometimes, however, this seems to happen in total abstraction from awareness of historical developments which have taken place in Biblical scholarship in interpretation and recognition of the varieties of language. On the other hand, apologists for faith are sometimes so confident that they stand in an ongoing tradition, that they simply beg all the questions of whether they can be said to share the *same* belief as their ancestors. Both those who deny and those who affirm constantly ignore psychological or sociological accounts of their belief, and those who are concerned with faith too often completely neglect other areas of belief. If we manage to map out in outline the whole territory of the discussion, this may make subsequent small-scale exploration easier, or put it in better perspective.

DISCUSSION QUESTIONS

Which of the questions raised in this chapter seem to you the most important ones at the outset of a discussion on religious belief?

8

Are there other questions which you would add to those raised here?

FOR FURTHER READING

F. R. Tennant, *The Nature of Belief*. The Christian Challenge Series.

2

THE QUESTION OF EVIDENCE I

The spacious firmament on high,
With all the blue ethereal sky,
And spangled heavens, a shining frame,
Their great Original proclaim.
The unwearied sun from day to day
Does his Creator's power display,
And publishes to every land
The works of an almighty hand.

JOSEPH ADDISON (1672–1719)

This world, for aught he knows, is very faulty and imperfect, compared to a superior standard, and was only the first rude essay of some infant deity who afterwards abandoned it, ashamed of his lame performance: it is the work only of some dependent, inferior deity, and is the object of derision to his superiors: it is the production of old age and dotage in some superannuated deity, and ever since his death has run on at adventures from the first impulse and active force which it received from him.

DAVID HUME *Dialogues concerning Natural Religion* (1761)

Occasionally courts have to settle the question of whether a child can be taken as the inheritor of parental fortunes in the absence of conclusive evidence that the parents have died. It is always a delicate business. There are no reliable deathbed witnesses, no substantiated death certificates, no exhumable graves. All possible avenues of contact must be checked. Time must be allowed to lapse. But if, after many years, no contrary evidence is found, the parents may be presumed to be dead.

Suppose one had set up a court to decide whether or not the world was the independent and self-sufficient inheritor of its religious past. Can God be presumed dead? Of course, in the case of God, being presumed dead would be tantamount to

10

'presumed never to have been alive'. Gods of good pedigree are not susceptible to death, and it is easier to believe that they have never really existed than that they have actually lived and actually died.

To encourage a little courtroom cut and thrust, let us imagine that this is not just a question of civil law. If God is dead, or was never alive, the Church is guilty of fraud. The world has been denied its autonomy, cheated of its inheritance by trustees who have enjoyed handling its fortune for it. Either by deliberate malice or by culpable negligence, they have not made clear the disappearance of the gods. Criminal proceedings are therefore appropriate.

Many witnesses could be called, and the selection here is restricted to a few key parties to the dispute. Readers, as jurors, must be aware that even witnesses who are trying to speak the truth have a limited perspective on the issues. They too must be assessed, and the extracts of cross-questioning recorded below are merely a starting point for the jury's deliberations.

PROSECUTION WITNESSES

PROSECUTOR Professor Higgle, would you tell the Court your profession?

HIGGLE I am a geneticist.

PROSECUTOR How does your competence in other scientific fields match up to your reputation in genetics?

HIGGLE Well, of course, things move so fast in various fields these days, one can't really keep up with all the specialists. But I trust I have a fairly coherent grasp of the major developments in most fields, if only in outline.

PROSECUTOR Would you care to give us a rough picture of how you see the character of the world, looking at it as a modern scientist.

HIGGLE That's a tall order. But let me indicate the points most relevant to this case. In the last decades we have been able to map exactly how man evolved from the basic primordial matter, the hydrogen and helium which are the original stuff of the universe. We can reconstruct how the process must have gone on,

11

through the formation of solids to the first emergence of organic life, and on to the evolution of man.

PROSECUTOR   Excuse me, Professor Higgle, are you saying there are no gaps in the process, no 'missing links'?

HIGGLE   That's right. The development is quite continuous and natural, given the original situation. And what's more, it all hangs together. The minutest particles, where we have to speak of 'matter-energy' rather than matter in motion, the vast cosmic energy concentrations which astrophysicists study, the detailed life of our own planet—all of them belong in one vast network of interrelationships. There is nothing foreign to the life of our world. The galaxies, the bacteria, the neutrinos, the people are all part of a huge interlocking jigsaw puzzle which makes one intelligible picture.

PROSECUTOR   You mean we don't need to posit any special intervention from outside the natural order to explain how organic life arose, or how conscious beings emerged?

HIGGLE   No, we don't. The increasing complexity of matter at one level explains how things emerge on new levels of organization. For example a certain degree of development in molecular structure leads to the point where matter can reproduce itself, that is to the level of organic life. But the activity of molecules in a tadpole is just the same sort of thing as the activity of molecules in a rock. Then a certain complexity of organic life produces a situation where a being can 'consciously' interact with its environment, instead of just interacting with it chemically or biologically. At that point we talk about the emergence of intelligence, but again, the activity of brain molecules doesn't involve some special unknown force which isn't there in the activity of molecules in the big toe. Given the whole reproductive process, the fact of 'natural selection' and the DNA code, man's emergence to consciousness is quite intelligible in view of his biological antecedents.

PROSECUTOR   Are you saying that consciousness is nothing but complex events in animal brain cells?

HIGGLE   No, not 'nothing but'. It seems to be invariably accompanied by events in brain cells, and possibly affected or even determined by such events. But to speak of 'consciousness' is to use a term which belongs on the level of awareness or agency. It can't be reduced to talk of brain cells. In the same way 'breathing' can't be adequately described in terms of atoms and molecules, though physicists could describe molecular behaviour concomitant with breathing and necessary for it. But breathing is a different sort of thing. As I think, a whole mass of activated tissue is doing various things in my skull. But even though I know that, I am not immediately aware of myself *as* complex activated tissue. I am aware of myself as a conscious agent, a centre of a world of experience, someone relating and related to, a self. It's rather like the poster which makes an appeal for crippled children by saying, 'He doesn't know what it is to jump puddles'. Well, of course, in one sense he *does*. He sees his friends do it. He may even understand how their muscles work. But none of that gives him the feel of puddle-jumping. You need a new language for the 'inside' experience.

PROSECUTOR But this awareness does not require any kind of outside interference in the process of nature, nothing like the implanting of a soul for instance?

HIGGLE Oh no, nothing like that.

PROSECUTOR Thank you, Professor Higgle. That will be all.

DEFENCE Professor Higgle, you said earlier, 'The development is quite continuous and natural, given the original situation'. Do you want to stop there?

HIGGLE I beg your pardon?

DEFENCE Why should you take as 'given' anything so staggering as a mass of hydrogen and helium with the potential to become the present world? Where did this original stuff come from? How do you explain it?

HIGGLE Well, we're not quite sure how it began. The scientific preference at the moment suggests a massive cosmic explosion thousands of millions of years ago. But possibly matter-energy has been constantly dilating and contracting for ever and ever.

DEFENCE But why should there be such an explosion in the first place? Why should there be time or space or matter or energy? Why should it all start? Doesn't it need explaining?

HIGGLE Well, I don't think I can answer that as a scientist. In fact, I'm not sure that I understand what you're asking. As far as I'm concerned there just *is* space-time, and there just *is* matter-energy. I start there. I can't even think what it could mean for that not to be the case. It's inconceivable. It wouldn't even be a different sort of world. It would be no world at all.

DEFENCE But why should there be a world at all?

HIGGLE I don't understand the question. Why shouldn't there be?

DEFENCE So you concede some sort of mystery about the origin of the world's existence.

HIGGLE Well, I think you're putting words into my mouth. I expect we'll find out in time whether it was a big bang or not. But beyond that I think it's just the basic fact that there is a world. It just so happens there is.

DEFENCE Thank you, Professor Higgle. You may step down.

PROSECUTOR Dr Trampett. You are a historian with considerable archaeological experience. Is that correct?

TRAMPETT Yes, correct.

PROSECUTOR Professor Higgle has just been saying there is no 'gap' in the world of natural science where God has to be brought in to explain why things are such and such a way. Are there gaps in history?

TRAMPETT You mean, are there things which historians can't explain?

PROSECUTOR Yes.

TRAMPETT Well, of course there are. It's mainly because unexplained things need explaining that historians take up history. So much is fascinating and quite obscure: why wars started,
14

why civilizations declined, how power changed hands—that kind of thing.

PROSECUTOR   Would you ever explain these things by bringing in God?

TRAMPETT   Oh no, certainly not. You can't bring in God to explain things. That's a kind of historical short-circuiting. No, there must be natural explanations, the complexity of human motives, the variety of social interaction, the coincidences of people picking up other people's ideas, the tensions in a culture. All these sort of things explain why events happen. Natural human causes, that's our business.

PROSECUTOR   What about the Biblical period?

TRAMPETT   Well, it's continuous with what went before and after and roundabout. I mean you don't write Greek history by talking about how Zeus did things in fifth century B.C. Athens. Of course what people *believed* about Zeus affected to some extent what happened to them. And what Jews and Christians believe about God has sometimes affected their history. But it's their *beliefs* which cause things to happen. You don't need to bring God into it.

PROSECUTOR   Thank you, Dr Trampett. Your witness ...

DEFENCE   You say you needn't bring God into it, Dr Trampett, but do you need to keep him out of it?

TRAMPETT   What do you mean?

DEFENCE   When you say there *must* be natural explanations, is that not a bit dogmatic? Why couldn't there be supernatural explanations? And if people believe things, couldn't it be because God caused their beliefs? I mean, if Moses believed God spoke to him, couldn't that have been because God did speak to him?

TRAMPETT   Well, it could have been, I suppose. That's a matter of personal opinion, but it seems to me there's no way of proving it one way or another. And so from the point of view of explaining things it's irrelevant. At least in principle we can understand how Moses came to have the conviction that God

15

spoke to him (if there ever was a man called Moses, and he's not just a folk-hero). That's enough to explain why things developed as they did.

DEFENCE   Well, it may be enough to give one explanation, but might not God's speaking to him be a fuller explanation of what happened? Are you not as prejudiced as the natural scientist who takes the world for granted and says it doesn't need God to explain it because he can show how it works? Isn't it doctrinaire to deny that God ever acts in history? I mean how else could you explain the extraordinary series of coincidences which led to the spread of Christianity?

TRAMPETT   Well, in a way the spread of Christianity is no more a coincidence than anything else; in fact one can explain it fairly convincingly in terms of the cultural situation in the Middle East. Of course, in one sense history is full of coincidences. Things just happen next. People just happen to meet people. The contingency of it is part of the fascination. But there's no reason to attribute selected coincidences to God. You can never show how things would have been different if God hadn't acted, since you can't re-run a piece of history with different variables the way you can repeat a chemistry experiment without the chlorine. History only happens once. And since you can't say how things would have been any different without God, he's historically irrelevant. You're never forced to say: 'That was *such* an odd event, it must have been God'. Looked at one way, they're equally explicable, because human nature seems to be fairly constant, even in its unpredictability.

DEFENCE   But how do you explain people having ideas of God?

TRAMPETT   I don't know why in general they do, if they do. I suppose psychologists or anthropologists could tell you more about that. But we can often explain how particular ideas of God change. For instance, Jews come in contact with Zoroastrians and certain ideas rub off, or create defensive reactions. Or a particular man meets others who persuade him to become a Christian. Historians can't generalize about belief; they can only trace the origins of this one or that one.

DEFENCE   But you're still assuming they can't have a super-

16

natural origin. That's not being historical; it's being doctrinaire.

TRAMPETT No, it's not; it's imposing a professional limit. A doctor may believe that God sends sickness and health to people, but *as* a doctor he assumes that there are natural causes; he looks for symptoms, makes a diagnosis and writes a prescription. If a historian has a certain religious viewpoint he may believe that God is somehow responsible for everything that happens, but that has to be bracketed out from his professional activity. It's medieval to see God bobbing in and out of human history.

DEFENCE What about well-documented miracles? Are they not historically established?

TRAMPETT It depends what you mean. Many things have happened which have been called miracles by the people involved. For some of them there are 'natural' historical explanations, for others there are not, at least at present. But to judge that they are in fact miracles is not the historian's job; it's the theologian's. The historian can look at the character of the evidence, the intellectual and cultural background of the witnesses, and the religious context. But how does he judge whether something's an act of God or an act of Allah? If he seems to have a sufficient explanation in natural terms for most events, he is entitled to assume that a natural explanation may be forthcoming in time even for the extraordinary ones.

DEFENCE But aren't you again ruling out the *possibility* of miracles in advance?

TRAMPETT Professionally, yes. I find that in my own present experience it always makes sense to look for natural explanations. I find when I look at history that the gaps which people allowed for the supernatural have closed. Plagues which used to be seen as supernatural visitations came to be recognized as natural phenomena. The rise and death of kings are seen as events of power politics, not as the work of divine subcommittees. The flourishing and decay of faiths, the triumph of doctrines, the extermination of heretics are as convincingly explicable on human grounds as the impact of Napoleon on the

French Constitution. I see no reason to suppose that things were different in the past.

DEFENCE   Why not? Might God not have acted in the past in ways which he no longer employs?

TRAMPETT   Possibly, but it's easier to explain the different assumptions about miracles by a cultural shift than by a basic change in God's ways of working, I'd have thought ... but I'm no theologian.

DEFENCE   And why should 'being easier' make an argument likely to be true?

TRAMPETT   I don't know. But there's something compelling about intellectual economy.

DEFENCE   There might be something compelling about buying size fives because they're cheaper than size sixes and you can actually get your feet into them. But the economy might be distorting. May your intellectual economy not in fact be *over*-simplifying the world?

TRAMPETT   I take that risk.

DEFENCE   Thank you. That is all for the moment.

DISCUSSION QUESTIONS

Do you expect either science or history to be able to prove God's existence? If so, how?

Do you think that either science or history could, in principle or in fact, disprove God's existence? If so, how?

FOR FURTHER READING

A. G. N. Flew and A. McIntyre, ed., *New Essays in Philosophical Theology*, Chapter IV. S.C.M. Press.
C. A. Coulson, *Science and Christian Belief*. Fontana.
Van A. Harvey, *The Historian and the Believer*. S.C.M. Press.

3

THE QUESTION OF EVIDENCE II

'I do not want to argue,' said the black girl. 'I want to know why, if you really made the world, you made it so badly.'

'Badly!' cried The Nailer. 'Ho! You set yourself up to call me to account! Who are you, pray, that you should criticize me? Can you make a better world yourself? Just try; that's all. Try to make one little bit of it. For instance, make a whale. Put a hook in its nose and bring it to me when you have finished. Do you realize, you ridiculous little insect, that I not only made the whale, but made the sea for him to swim in? The whole mighty ocean, down to its bottomless depths and up to the top of the skies. You think that was easy I suppose. You think you could do it better yourself. I tell you what, young woman: you want the conceit taken out of you. You couldn't make a mouse; and you set yourself up against me, who made a megatherium. You couldn't make a pond; and you dare talk to me, the maker of the seven seas. You will be ugly and old and dead in fifty years, whilst my majesty will endure for ever; and here you are taking me to task as if you were my aunt. You think, don't you, that you are better than God? What have you to say to that argument?'

'It isn't an argument; it's a sneer,' said the black girl. 'You don't seem to know what an argument is.'

G. B. SHAW *The Black Girl in Search of God*

DEFENCE WITNESSES

DEFENCE Mr Dickery, you are a philosopher. Have you any special interest in religion?

DICKERY Well, I specialize in metaphysics and epistemology,

19

so I'm rubbing shoulders with questions of religious philosophy all the time.

DEFENCE   Would you please indicate briefly to the jury what 'metaphysics' and 'epistemology' are.

DICKERY   I'm not sure that I can give you uncontroversial definitions, since philosophers disagree about metaphysics as much as artists disagree about art. But let me try. Some things about the world could obviously be different without it being a radically different world. You might have red hair instead of black hair. Or the population of Great Britain might be 56,000,000 instead of 53,000,000. Or your nephew might have died at birth. Or water might have had a boiling point at sea level of 95°C. These are contingent facts about the world which particular sciences explore and explain. But suppose there were no such things as people; or suppose time could be reversed; or things could stop being themselves and start again. Then the world would be so very different that it would seem to be another reality altogether. Metaphysics is the branch of philosophy which, traditionally, concerns itself with the most basic structures of reality, the things without which this world could not *be* this world; like time, space, cause and effect, identity, substance. Or, if it's misleading to talk about these as 'things', it explores the concepts which are basic for us in framing our manifold experiences. Is that clear?

DEFENCE   Well, it sounds very abstract. But tell us about epistemology.

DICKERY   That's not so hard. It's the branch of philosophy dealing with the criteria for knowledge.

DEFENCE   What sort of knowledge?

DICKERY   Any sort. How do I know that the external world really exists? How do I know other people have minds? Can I know the past or the future, and how could I justify either claim? Have I good grounds for claiming to know I am the same person today as I was yesterday? Can I know what's right and wrong, and how? Of course some of these questions run into issues of metaphysics or conceptual definitions, but epis-
20

temology is specially concerned with a systematic account of how we justify claims to *know*.

DEFENCE Well then, Mr Dickery, I'd like your professional opinion on some of the points that have arisen so far. You say metaphysicians discuss cause and effect?

DICKERY That's right.

DEFENCE What do you make, then, of the suggestions of Higgle and Trampett that the world could be explained by natural means?

DICKERY I think the question needs to be clearer. If Higgle means that he can explain some detail X about the world in terms of other details A, B, C, then I take his word for it as a scientist and a gentleman. And if Trampett says A happened because O and P happened, I trust his historical judgement. But when philosophers have said that the world isn't self-explanatory they haven't been talking about explaining why this *detail* is like this or that. They've been talking about why *any* of it exists. I think you were pushing Trampett in that direction. Heidegger summed it up by asking 'Why is there something, and not nothing?' Higgle couldn't, as a scientist, explain that.

DEFENCE Can metaphysicians explain it?

DICKERY Sometimes they've thought they could. Traditionally, they've talked of a First Cause. That wasn't one thing within the series of finite causes and effects, but the undergirding of the whole series.

DEFENCE And what caused the First Cause?

DICKERY By definition the First Cause has no antecedent cause. It is self-originating. Nothing precedes it or gives it being.

DEFENCE Does that explain the world?

DICKERY Well, I'm inclined myself to think it doesn't, in any really informative sense of 'explain'. But I think it's a way of registering the conviction that the world is *not* self-explanatory. No matter how much we understand its *workings*, the *existence* of the world is amazing.

21

DEFENCE   And how are God and the First Cause connected?

DICKERY   One main Western Christian tradition has identified them. Thomas Aquinas in the thirteenth century believed that any rational being must concede a First Cause, and that Christians called that First Cause 'God' (and then had more inside information on his character to fill out the picture).

DEFENCE   Thank you, Mr Dickery. Your witness.

PROSECUTOR   Mr Dickery, let us go back to the question you raised. 'Why is there anything and not nothing?' Why shouldn't there be?

DICKERY   What do you mean?

PROSECUTOR   Why shouldn't there just happen to be a world? Wouldn't it be more astonishing if it wasn't there? Why should one not see this kind of question itself as bizarre and just accept the world as given.

DICKERY   'Given' presupposes a giver.

PROSECUTOR   That's just a figure of speech. I mean 'given' only in the sense that we find it there, we don't invent it.

DICKERY   Perhaps to some extent it's a matter of how it strikes you. Obviously we are here, in a world. That's where we find ourselves, and we can take it for granted. But when you go down a staircase and find there's a seventh step when you expected six, or you find yourself in the free fall of going to sleep, or someone dies, then the thought may come, 'But *none* of it might have been here. There was no necessity for any of it.' Then you don't take it for granted. Its solidity is amazing.

PROSECUTOR   That's mere circumstance of mood and temperament. It doesn't support any *logical* demand for an explanation. If the world amazes you, that says more about you than about the world. Anyway, you admit that you don't explain anything by talking of a First Cause.

DICKERY   I certainly don't think I give you another stage back in a causal sequence of finite events, like saying 'The loss of the roof tiles was explained by high winds'. It's more like putting

22

the world into another perspective altogether. You know how sometimes you revise your whole opinion of a relationship to someone. All the details are as they were. But you feel as if you see the person 'in focus', in a new light. People who talk of a First Cause seem to me to be unable to focus the world as 'takeable for granted'. They focus it only as needing to be explained.

PROSECUTOR Then it's precisely the same for them to talk of a First Cause as for Indian mythology to talk of the tortoise which supports the elephant which supports the world?

DICKERY Precisely the same, in my opinion.

PROSECUTOR You're a very untypical philosopher, are you not?

DICKERY What's typical?

PROSECUTOR I'd have thought most contemporary philosophers would distrust such metaphysics, and regard Heidegger in particular as talking nonsense.

DICKERY Well, it may be my contacts with non Anglo-Saxons! Or with theologians! But I persist in finding it reasonable to be surprised that anything exists.

PROSECUTOR Let us move on then from the question of there being a world at all to the question of what *kind* of world it is. We disagree about the *fact* of the world's existence being a basis for belief in God. Surely its *character* is the strongest possible evidence against God.

DICKERY Is that not too bold a statement?

PROSECUTOR Come, come, Mr Dickery. Amid wastes and wastes of silicon, in enormous aeons of time, here is one planet where life can be sustained, for a few millenia. Within this one world, vast numbers of creatures and even species have lived only to die out. The survival of some depends on the destruction of others. Men are born with aggressions and needs which, combined with the distribution of world resources, load their future in the direction of hostility with their fellows. They are liable to natural disaster, disease, fear, loneliness, age, corruption and

23

death. Is it not easier to believe there is no God than to try to square a God with such a world?

DICKERY   It may be easier. That does not affect its truth. Besides, you seem to me to elaborate only one side of the picture. Men are also liable to beauty, health, laughter, love, moral endeavour, freedom and hope.

PROSECUTOR   Yes, but that's surely the least you would expect in God's world. It's the other side which puts belief under pressure. That the world and its inhabitants should be at all marred is surprising if God made them. That it should be so thoroughly marred reduces to absurdity the notion of a good divine Creator.

DICKERY   Well, really, I feel I have no professional competence to go further. My religious convictions I can defend as an amateur. As a philosopher I find the evidence for God more in the fact that the world exists than in its character.

PROSECUTOR   Thank you, Mr Dickery. You may step down.

DEFENCE   Dr Crunch, you are a theologian and a pastor. Would you care to outline to the jury how as a theologian you would defend God against the sceptical questions of the prosecution?

CRUNCH   No.

DEFENCE   I beg your pardon.

CRUNCH   It isn't my job to defend God against anything.

DEFENCE   But you must acknowledge the problem.

CRUNCH   Indeed, but the problem is more the inadequacy of human ideas of God than anything in God himself.

DEFENCE   Then would you care to give some idea of how a more adequate idea might be formulated?

CRUNCH   Yes, indeed. People sometimes talk as if it was proper to complain about the state of the world to God as one complains to a shoemaker about a badly made shoe. Two things can be said about that. In the first place, within the image of God as personal, there has to be room for his recognition of the freedom and responsibility of his creation. In those terms, in a

24

way, he gives *us* the world to make; and to undo the pain and chaos we make would be to unman us, like a parent saying to a child just learning to tie shoelaces, 'No, No! I'll do it. You're so clumsy at it.'

Secondly, to say 'God made the world' is to use only an image, a picture, a model, an analogy. There's a tentative, provisional character about it, since we can't speak literally of things happening *before* or outside space-time, yet creation can't be an event *in* space-time. The real point in making the statement isn't to describe a cosmic event, like God striking in thin air the match which caused the big bang. It's affirming a commitment to a certain way of living in the world.

DEFENCE What do you mean?

CRUNCH Well, it's very complex. But let me give some examples. If I say 'God made the world' it means I cannot regard it as a wholly alien environment, the way some religions find it a loathsome cage of the spirit. The world is a place of true life for me. At the same time there is an incompleteness about it; my life cannot be fully defined in terms of what happens in the world, because God is not the world, and my life in the end can only be understood with God as its horizon. Still, because God is its horizon, I can live life as worth living. I can trust that love is stronger than hate. I can see I only make sense in a community without limits. Saying 'God made the world' is a shorthand commitment to all that.

DEFENCE Could you explain what 'God is its horizon' means?

CRUNCH Not exactly. Certainly it's not something which can be described or demonstrated on neutral ground. It's more like finding someone's lovable by loving him. You can't really show a dispassionate observer that someone's lovable. The assertion only makes sense among people who do love him. With 'God is the world's horizon' it's something like that. People who do trust that love is stronger than hate, who open up to the stranger, who embrace life even in its darkness—they do find that their limited discovery suggests or demands a fuller possibility of openness and love. 'God' is the name by which men acknowledge the unthinkable, unlimited, promiscuous, prodigal resources of free life which they experience.

25

DEFENCE   Thank you, Dr Crunch. Your witness.

PROSECUTOR   Dr Crunch, you suggest that God gives man responsibility for the world.

CRUNCH   Yes.

PROSECUTOR   But surely man isn't responsible for much of it. The laws of geophysics and astraphysics, the DNA code and his brain chemistry. These things make man what he is. He doesn't make them.

CRUNCH   No, but in a sense he transcends them. He can learn about his own nature and the nature of the world, and has freedom and power to act on that basis. He has the future of the planet in his own hands.

PROSECUTOR   But that's a very recent development, and very limited still. Surely God has to be held responsible for all the poor impotents who've been swallowed up by earthquakes and for untreatable insanity and death.

CRUNCH   I admit that's a problem I can't solve. Given the original molecules, I take Professor Higgle's word for it that this whole world was bound to emerge to the point where human freedom could change it. Now just how this reality called 'God' relates to all these molecules I'm not sure. I don't want to say he doesn't relate at all, because that seems to commit the old Gnostic heresy that God has nothing to do with matter. On the other hand, I don't want to suggest that he shunts molecules around, certainly not selected molecules, interfering with a process which would otherwise go differently.

PROSECUTOR   Then isn't God really redundant as an active force? He's just an idea.

CRUNCH   Well, he isn't an active force in the sense of impersonal energy bombarding the world. But that doesn't mean he's just an idea. When I encounter another person and change him and am changed by him, something really happens. But it can't be described in terms of a mutual effect our molecules have on each other. It seems that talk of God only makes sense on the level of personal encounter.

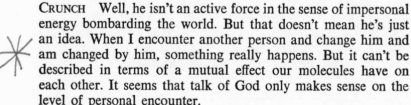

PROSECUTOR But personal encounter depends on molecules. No molecules, no encounter. So how do you encounter God?

CRUNCH Well, what I call 'encountering God' is growing in this active conviction that I am only made sense of by a love which has no limits.

PROSECUTOR But if God inspires this conviction, he is shoving molecules around, because convictions mean things going on in your brain cells.

CRUNCH Yes, but not their manipulation. When I 'make you angry' your anger has corresponding brain activity. But you are angry because I provoked *you*. That's quite different from 'being angry' because I directly stimulate areas of your brain. God's influence is more like the interaction of a person with people than some quasi-physical stimulus.

PROSECUTOR But can you ever show, even in that sense, that it's *God* who causes your ideas or convictions? I mean how do you know they're caused by God rather than by other people, or books you've read, or a good dinner, or the state of your glands?

CRUNCH No, I can't show it. God doesn't come, at least not to me, as a separate individual with 'God' on his T-shirt. But through people, or books, or even sometimes a good dinner, I find mediated this conviction—it feels more like this *awareness* —that the world has its life in relation to a reality which transcends it.

PROSECUTOR But that might be your imagination, or your private construction of things, or even your indigestion. It might be.

CRUNCH Yes, it might be. But I hope it isn't.

PROSECUTOR Thank you, Dr Crunch. You may step down.

DEFENCE SUMMING UP My Lord, ladies and gentlemen of the jury. You will, I trust, appreciate the subtlety of the defence case. We offer no crude demonstrations of a supernatural being, no bangs so big that they coerce belief, no gaps so gaping that they *demand* a divine explanation. Instead, we bring to your

27

attention an accumulation of many factors which make the case for belief more plausible than not.

Is it, I ask you, really convincing to suppose that mere random whirling of subatomic particles could by sheer statistical chance result in a world as complex and highly organized as this? Is it convincing to explain by natural selection and sheer accident all these aspects of man which have no bearing on his evolutionary survival, his capacity for laughter, his compulsion to write music, his delight in colour, his power of self-sacrifice? Can coincidence explain the many times when lives have been radically changed by totally unpremeditated meetings with people whose existence was undreamt of? Can the survival of the Church against all the pressures and onslaughts of time and culture be explained without reference to some kind of Providence? Does the fact that man is staggered by the sheer 'is-ness' of things, the fact that he quests indomitably for meaning in existence, not suggest a depth to reality which cannot be exhausted by naturalistic description? Why are we here? Why is the world here? How does man find the sense of the numinous so frequently documented in human existence? By what power does he achieve ecstasy? Can all the manifold religious experience of mankind be dismissed as fantasy or indigestion?

Taken singly, ladies and gentlemen of the jury, no one of these questions will take the weight of the whole defence case. But held together, they indicate an area of human questioning which can be answered only by religious belief. The niceties of dogma do not concern us here. But I trust you will by now be persuaded that only some form of religious assertion can do justice to the many rumours of angels which emerge from our existence.

PROSECUTION SUMMING UP My Lord, members of the jury. My colleague's winsomeness of rhetoric is surpassed only by his poverty of logic. Let us look with some detachment at the testimony before us. We have a scientist who tells us that there is no break in the seamless robe of scientific explanation. We have a historian who insists that historical research cannot invoke the hypothesis of an intervening God. We have a philosopher whose main plank is that the sheer existence of the world needs explanation. And we have a theologian who has attempted to redefine what it means to believe God made the world—a subtlety which will not, I trust, seduce the jury from its inevitable conclusion.

Let us rescrutinize the defence case.

Dickery bases his whole argument on the appeal of the emotive suggestion that man's cosmic wonder demands an absolute explanation. Not how the world is, but *that* it is, he suggests, is a fact which will not lie down and just be the case. But then what is he saying? By implication that it is *not* just the case. By implication that the world is planned, providential, purposeful, moving towards a goal. But *look* at it. Does the extent of its disorder not reduce the hypothesis to absurdity?

Question by rhetorical question, the defence can be beaten down. Could a planner with any say in the origins of matter and any sweetness of imagination allow a system so wasteful of space and time, and so cavalier in its regard for individual life? Is it more credible that an empty cosmos has been devised for the sake of this minute planet which has come and will go, than that we are a freak of infinitesimal statistical chance? Are the downs of history, the disasters of human encounter, the blighting of life by life not sufficient counterpoise to the 'providential' situations which the defence detects? Are man's ecstasies, visions and questions not functions of his own complex nature rather than promptings of an external reality?

Fortunately for the prosecution, the theologian has virtually sold the religious pass. Belief in God as creator, we are told, is not belief in a supernatural fact. It is a commitment to certain attitudes to life. Does common sense not wince at such slipperiness? Were the founders of the faith merely committing themselves to certain styles of life? Did they not believe that the existence and intervention of God were facts as brute as the existence and intervention of their own parents? One need not spend time demolishing Crunch's evasions. Commitment to contrary views of the world could equally be 'confirmed' by experience. All that either conviction proves is that men can see selectively and project grotesquely what chimes in with their initial convictions. To such belief evidence is irrelevant.

Let me remind you in closing, members of the jury, that we are debating whether the Church can offer any good grounds for religious belief on the basis of the existence or character of the world.

In the past, there were so many phenomena unexplained that men might, in good faith, postulate a divine, supernatural explanation of this or that. Now the gaps have closed. The natural world is vast enough, dense enough to hold in its own complex existence the answer to all our intelligible questions.

But those whose interest and security are vested in the religious past cannot face their own self-sufficiency nor allow yours. So we now have a 'defence' of belief to which no evidence is relevant, since it is a matter of arbitrary commitment.

Members of the jury, this façade of intellectually and morally crumbling argument barely disguises the fact that religious belief today has no foundations. There is no sound evidence for it, much against it. It stands at all, only because fear and prejudice would cheat the world of its proper autonomy, and exploit its weaker emotions. But if only men look clearly at the evidence, it will not stand long.

The prosecution rests.

DISCUSSION QUESTIONS

Are you more impressed by arguments from *how* the world is to the existence of God or by arguments from the sheer fact of its existence? Can you clarify your preference on this issue?

Do you think a stronger argument for God's existence or against it could be offered by concentrating on any other aspect of human existence than those considered here?

Which of the counsels do you judge to be fairer in his handling of the witnesses and their evidence?

FOR FURTHER READING

R. Hepburn, *Christianity and Paradox*, Chapters 9 and 10. C. A. Watts.

M. Buber, *I and Thou*. T. & T. Clark.

D. Hume, *Dialogues Concerning Natural Religion*. Hafner.

4

OTHER ARGUMENTS FOR BELIEF

> I know the special kind of life I like,
> What suits the most my idiosyncrasy
> Brings out the best of me and bears me fruit
> In power, peace, pleasantness, and length of days.
> I found that positive belief does this
> For me, and unbelief no whit of this.
>
> ROBERT BROWNING *Bishop Blougram's Apology*

The two previous chapters have not yet given rise to a verdict. They have merely suggested some of the evidence offered for or against the truth of belief, and presented two ways of reading that evidence. All kinds of evaluative questions remain to be asked. The kind of thing a wise judge might invite jurors to consider in his summing up: Was the evidence well-chosen? Were important areas of evidence for or against belief left out? Were the witnesses good witnesses, or were they biased? Were they bullied by the way questions were put? Did either counsel give proper weight to the opposition arguments? Did they both beg the question whether what they were talking about made sense, let alone whether it could be proved true or false? Did they even agree about what they *were* debating, or was one trying to deny what the other was never trying to affirm?

All these issues are still untidily open, but for the moment let us suspend judgement on them and move on to map another area in the discussion of belief.

Imagine two middle-aged ladies waking up on holiday on a morning when they've decided to go out for a full day's picnic. As they get up it's dry but overcast. All through the preceding week it's started off like this, and some days have ended with rain, while some have cleared to bright sun by midday. The official weather forecast, hedging its bets, suggests a possibility of sunny spells with a chance of heavy showers. Local wisdom refuses to be drawn further than, 'well, it could clear'. The friends have two options. One is to take raincoats and umbrellas, the other is to risk it, and leave them at home.

Suppose they have an argument on the matter. What they are disagreeing about is not whether rain is likely, since they both acknowledge that it may come or it may not. One urges the taking of umbrellas, because if it rains you can get pretty wet out in the open, and they aren't all that cumbersome to carry. The other suspects with William Blake that 'prudence is a rich ugly old maid courted by incapacity' and abjures such spinsterish caution. The prospect of walking untrammelled, she insists, is worth the risk, and there are always dry clothes to change into, even if it rains.

Some believers think their dispute with non-believers is more like an argument about whether to carry umbrellas than like a debate as to whether it will rain. They may not be the most convinced defenders of the faith, in that they recognize that the evidence *is* ambiguous. They don't claim that the world unmistakably shows God's existence, but rather that as far as evidence goes, it's an open question. So much they concede to the agnostic.

It is, however, possible for believers who are modest about the evidence to be confident about the merits of believing, to be sure that belief is better than doubt, and to offer some kind of reason for their conviction. In this chapter we shall air some of the arguments offered in defence of believing where the evidence is acknowledged to be inconclusive.

One classic statement comes in the writing of Blaise Pascal, the seventeenth-century Frenchman, who wrote a 'defence of true religion'. In this, he conducts a sort of running argument on the question of belief. At one point he has come to the conclusion that reason cannot settle the question of God's existence. He may exist or he may not. 'What', then asks Pascal, 'will you wager?' He rules out the possibility of refusing to opt for one or other belief, and goes on:

Wager you must, there is no option, you have embarked on it. So which will you have. Come, since you must choose, let us see what concerns you least. You have two things to lose:

32

truth and good, and two things to stake, your reason and your will, your knowledge and your happiness. And your nature has two things to shun: error and misery. Your reason does not suffer by your choosing one more than the other, for you must choose. That is one point cleared. But your happiness? Let us weigh gain and loss in calling heads that God is. Reckon these two chances: if you win, you win all; if you lose, you lose naught. Then do not hesitate, wager that He is.

Pascal's gamble is really an extreme form of an argument from prudence. Admittedly he allows that if there were overriding evidence on either side it would be irresponsible to ignore it. But no such evidence is available. You are therefore rationally free to opt for either, and the main consideration must be where you have more to lose. If there is no God, and presumably no life after death, you may in fact be wrong to believe, but it won't do you much harm. You won't even have the pain of ever knowing your belief was wrong, since there won't *be* any you to realize it. On the other hand, if God does exist, you stand to gain a good deal by believing, and your disbelief may cost you eternal life and happiness.

Pascal's suggestion of course begs a question which we still have to discuss, namely whether believing is something you can *choose* to do. Can one decide to adopt a belief the way one can decide to take an umbrella? Unless one can, there will be little point in discussing whether one should.

Obviously, however, Pascal thought he was recommending something which could be done, whether or not we would want to call it proper belief. A soldier before the battle of Blenheim is quoted as praying, 'O God, if there be a God, save my soul, if I have a soul'. One could presumably decide to speak such words, rather than to refrain from speaking them. One could practise habits of intended devotion, attend acts of public worship, explore the implications of belief, if it were true, get into the habit of asking how everyday events might look to the eyes of faith.

Our immediate question is whether Pascal's *reasons* for doing any of these things are good reasons. Is it a good argument for religious belief that you've everything to gain, and nothing to lose?

Certainly Pascal does not lack company. The Christian Church might well be embarrassed by the amount of popular evangelism which has exploited human fear and self-interest. At its crudest, this has taken the form of threats of hell or promises of heaven, and saving one's spiritual bacon has been offered as a main enticement to belief.

One need not be a non-believer to be appalled by such appeals. *Any* God petty and vindictive enough to punish non-believers seems grotesquely unworshipful. More specifically, any convincing reconciliation between such a concept of the character of God and a Christian *gospel* is impossible. Christianity would then be bad news. Absorption with one's own fate seems a stunting and narrowing concern in any human being, far less a mark of admirers of an unself-preoccupied Jesus.

Further, the testimony of believers in many faiths is that any notion of 'external' reward and punishment disappears as understanding and love mature. Belief is not a pill to be sweetened, a step to be taken for the sake of some goal beyond, an umbrella to be lumbered with in order to remain eschatologically dry. The only *reason* for belief, from the believer's perspective, is its content, the exuberant goodness of the reality the believer believes in. If such testimony is taken seriously, religious belief cannot really be a spiritual parallel to taking out an insurance policy. That is not because prudence is *necessarily* deplored as a human motive; it is merely that it is incompatible with the absence of self-concern which marks any real religious devotion. Even if believing is, in some sense, for one's good, that cannot be *why* one does it. Only people of the cynicism of Oscar Wilde characters can recommend falling in love because of the effect that has on the lover.

The point is obvious when the argument for belief is as crude as some traditional pie-in-the-sky promises or fire-and-brimstone threats suggest. It is, however, a more subtle appeal to the outcome which is made by Pascal or by the somewhat Pascalian hero of *Bishop Blougram's Apology*. The outcome of belief offered as a reasonable ground for accepting it is, in such cases, not merely future security but present fruitfulness. What the most seductive of the commercials cannot provide faith can:

confidence, steadiness, energy, peace, joy, hope, maturity and true enjoyment of life. Is the effect belief has on the immediate life of the believer not a good enough argument for its adoption?

In the first place, it is hard to plot the actual correlation between belief and character. Some of the alleged fruit looks pretty sour and maggot-ridden, though opinions on the matter are likely to be impressionistic rather than based on scientific investigation. But impressions may matter, and religious believers often appear, in literature for example, as authoritarian and conservative, afraid of life, puritanical, clichéd, morbidly concerned about their own spiritual temperature, hypocritical and complacent.

Generalization is, of course, impossible in so complex an area, and even head-counting is of little value. Suppose even that some believers *are* more open than the average man, more free, more relaxed, more full of laughter. Suppose one occasionally encounters in them an enviable sanity and balance and generosity towards life. Suppose they *do* seem to live more vividly than their neighbours, or to be more alert to the injustices of their society. What does that prove? Such qualities are relatively rare in men and women of any creed. They occur too often, one suspects, in non-religious people, or in those of various faiths, for any particular belief system to be able to claim a monopoly of human excellence. Besides, it is very hard to show that someone is the man he is *because* of what he believes rather than in spite of it. People may live more maturely than they believe, or vice versa, with no sense of a discrepancy between the two. Those who can document changes of life clearly caused by changes in belief must be relatively rare.

It is always a theoretical option, of course, to distinguish between the effects of 'belief at its best' and the routine effects in common or garden cases. By that method one eliminates the problem of devout bigots, Christian racists and graceless do-gooders. One also eliminates, however, any basis for a *general* claim that believing has good effects on its believers, at least while the majority of the faithful are common or garden cases. A rule may survive exceptions; it cannot consist of exceptions.

It may be, though, that judgements about the justification of belief by its effects are not at all dependent on statistics. Someone might grant that people's lives are often impervious to the

35

brunt of their beliefs. He might recognize that lip-service can be paid to creeds without invalidating them, that the transformation of a life may be as slow and ragged a business as its first moulding was, even that the clientele longing for salvation may involve more morally crippled men than the average bus queue. Still, he may have encountered even one or two people who do convince him that their belief and their character hang together. He may find in them such a quality of life that he is compelled to take their belief seriously, and tempted to trust it, no matter how many addled versions of the same belief he has met.

This is not to say that a man could really have the hoped-for effect on his own character as a primary *motive* for believing, not if he really understood the difference between religious belief and moral re-armament. But if observers could say without irony, 'See how these Christians (or any other group) love one another', that *would* be some kind of rational argument for accepting the belief. It would be the rationale of Pragmatism[1] or Utilitarianism,[2] but that is a rationale.

In Browning's poem quoted at the beginning of this chapter, Bishop Blougram is debating with Mr Gigadibs the justification of his belief. Gigadibs is intellectually scrupulous, refusing any commitment beyond the strict evidence, and despising Blougram for his compromise, since the latter too admits doubt as a fair response to the evidence. Blougram vindicates himself by a subtle and expansive pragmatic defence of belief. The poem, of course, is a dramatic monologue, so one need not assume that Browning himself applauds his hero's views, but within the poem it is Gigadibs who emerges as a somewhat zealous, shrill, and shrivelled individual, while Blougram's defence of belief as an aid to 'the good life' is presented as realistic and emotionally more generous.

[1] Pragmatism is the philosophical position which holds that the truth of an assertion is established by the desirability of its effects, by its practical utility. Popularly it is understood as the view that 'the end justifies the means'.

[2] Utilitarianism is the ethical theory which contends that the effect of an action on the greatest happiness of the greatest number is the primary criterion of its morality. Thus, even if the belief were not true, a Utilitarian might still accept that it was *better* to encourage belief in what was untrue, than to insist in belief only in what was true.

36

Is it merely a matter of temperament that utilitarianism satisfies some people and not others, or can more be said? To some, all discussion of the truth of a belief is pointless, unless the effects of holding it are desirable. To others, no matter how desirable the effects, they are, as it were, fraudulently achieved on false pretences unless the belief is true in the first place. Certainly, there is something about most religious systems of belief which insists that the belief is effective only in so far as it is true. Indeed, in most contexts, to believe something *is* precisely to believe that it is true, independent of one's belief that it is. The debate is not about the possibility of believing something without believing it to be true; it is about the merits of holding that good effects of a belief are relevant or sufficient evidence of its truth.

On an initial commonsense level, the suggestion is ridiculous. If one were convinced that the universe is friendly, sustained by a will which is in the end for its good, this might have many amiable results. One might stop snarling at the things which seem insuperably distressing. One might be less strident in one's assertions or commitments, less competitive in one's relationships. All that might be agreed on as a desirable state of affairs. But the conviction might, logically, still be false. I might be just a haphazard cluster of atoms, hanging together for a certain length of time in a hostile or indifferent universe. My belief would then have the status of the 'noble myth' in Plato's *Republic* —it would not be true, but it would, if believed, work in certain socially desirable ways.

Another sort of argument appeals, not to the effects of believing that are visible to outsiders, but to its meaningfulness or inward force in the life of its exponents.

Anyone insisting that a belief's value to the believer *was* a criterion of its truth would in fact be redefining the concept of 'truth'. It might then be possible for the same belief to be true for you and false for me. It might be possible for contradictory beliefs to be simultaneously true for various people.

Such a view is sometimes hinted at almost as a matter of courtesy by members of one faith wishing to respect the faith of others, but not to share it. They deplore the black and white of old distinctions between pagan falsehood and Christian truth, and they have some hope that in the end it will turn out that

37

God has been working through various religious traditions.

It is much harder to work out a coherent intellectual framework for any such inclinations. The concept of truth we have inherited, especially from the empiricist scientific tradition, is that a thing is *either* true *or* it isn't. It may *seem* true to you and not to me, but it can't actually *be* true and false simultaneously. The whole assessment of evidence, the procedures of checking, presuppose that truth is something, in principle, objectively discoverable.

The main challenge to this view comes from the philosophical tradition known as Existentialism. Any outline of the whole network of Existentialist systems would require much more space and greater subtlety of discussion than this book allows. Simply, however, the Existentialist position on truth is that it is never a static relationship between states of affairs and propositions about them. Instead, whenever someone is involved in a situation he puts *himself* into his account of it. Whether his involvement is one of love, or horror, or boredom affects how he sees the situation. More than that, existentially, it is actually *part* of the situation, so that talk of 'the actual state of affairs' is an abstraction, unless the subjectivity of the speaker is also represented. But one person's 'situation' may be different from another's. In fact it is almost part of what it means to be a 'person' that your situation is different from another's. It follows therefore that the truth can never be spoken 'objectively', by abstracting some common factor from the various subjectivities which perceive it. It must be many-faceted and multiform.

Existentialism would certainly give no support to the view that truth could be established by quasi-statistical measurements of the effects of a belief. It would in that sense renounce pragmatism or utilitarianism. But it might accept that the truth of belief could only be known in the 'inwardness' of a situation, where the believer was involved in wrestling with its meaning for his own life. The question of choice and belief has to be more fully explored in the next chapter. At present we register as one element in any ongoing discussion this basic issue about what it means to say that a belief is true.

So far we have considered two possible justifications of belief in the absence of conclusive objective evidence. One was the strictly prudential appeal, which we suggested was an argument incompatible with any real understanding of the character of religious belief. The other was the argument from the impact of belief on the life of the believer, that being measured either objectively or subjectively.

When we considered the impressiveness of other people's lives as a good reason for believing, we were on the edge of another argument, an argument on the basis of trust. Some element of this is probably present in fact in any home where children grow up 'in the faith of their fathers'. Initially at least, a child may not think of asking for reasons why he should believe. At some stage, however, unless he is very sheltered, he will find a classmate who says there is no God, or meet a Muslim child, or start to ask his own questions. From this point on he knows that people believe different things, and it *is* a real problem why he should believe one rather than another. Depending on his relationship to his parents, he is liable to accept or reject their beliefs in proportion to his total trust or distrust of them. If he breaks with their beliefs, he may well accept the counter position of someone else he admires, someone who seems to him to know what life is about.

It is relatively rare, probably, for people to scrutinize every belief they are brought up in. Sometimes because they assume the beliefs are actually knowledge, the possibility of doubting never crosses their minds. Sometimes they know that it's a belief, but find it fits so well the shape of their world that there is no reason to challenge it. There are thousands of beliefs beyond his experience which a growing child is liable to accept from his parents: quite mundane ones about which brand of butter is best, or what kind of writing paper he should use; or on a larger scale, convictions that Conservative Party economics make most sense, that breaking the law is invariably wrong, that Christianity is the best religion.

With luck, a child has parents who equip him to sift and formulate his own beliefs, even if that means disagreeing with theirs. 'He's got to think for himself' they may say. With even more luck, his formal education may help him to be critical or sceptical about quite a lot of 'received opinion', though it may just as easily encourage more uncritical belief. Or events in his own life may toss up major obstacles to the plausibility of his inherited convictions. He may fall in love with the Secretary of

39

the local Labour Party, or find that the life of his child depends on his breaking the law, or be given as a Christmas present *The Misery of Christianity*.

Of course, if his beliefs are unshakeable enough, he can probably re-adjust. He can believe his love has been the victim of horrid propaganda in her youth, or that it is better his child should die than the law should be flouted, or that Kahl was really in the pay of the Communists.

Such inability to accept any counter evidence would suggest that the man's beliefs in this case were almost pathologically prejudiced. That is one end of a spectrum. At the other is the cool rational ideal of Enlightenment sanity, accepting no authority, but exposing all his beliefs to testing, and renouncing them where they fail. In between, however, are several positions where a man *could* be persuaded to change his mind, but so far hasn't been. He can't for one reason or another, check the truth of the belief for himself, so in the absence of conclusive evidence against it, he goes on trusting the people who told him.

Religious belief is a particularly crucial example of this phenomenon, because for most people it is mediated by a tradition. Very few people really go round the available faiths or ideologies assessing them all impartially. For one thing 'getting inside' any one tradition is a matter of such complexity that it is extremely hard even to understand an alien belief system. In addition, 'believing' for many adherents of a faith is something so amorphous that direct challenges to it are rare. People may assume in modesty that others have more first-hand, vivid religious experience than they do. Only if they are fairly sure that no such thing is possible will they suspect that others who make such claims are themselves misreading their experience, victims of a tradition which holds them prisoner. One has to be quite sophisticated to realize how hard it is to distinguish 'neat experience' from the learned ways of *describing* that experience. A man may have an uneasy feeling when he tells a lie to his wife. Brought up one way, he may record this experience in his diary as 'hearing the voice of conscience'; brought up in another he may say 'God showed me the error of my ways'. And he may have no *sense* that such accounts are interpretations of any sort. To him they are basic facts.

When this realization dawns on anyone assessing belief claims based on religious experience, the reaction may be a sense of quicksands. How can I compare the basis of one set of beliefs with that of another? Is the religious tradition I have trusted simply a chain of passed-on trust in other people's experiences? How can I know that the so-called 'community of experience' in my tradition is more than a common learned vocabulary, disguising the raggedness of actual first-hand experience. How, more basically, can I ever check that any experience is the same as someone else's. How do I know that when you eat pineapple you get the same taste as I do when I eat it?

Strictly speaking I don't; that is, I have no way of demonstrating my conviction that we both get the same taste. The outcome may seem a very nightmarish solipsism,[1] where I am trapped in my own experience, and cannot cross the boundary into anyone else's. On the other hand there is a measure of comfort in the success of cookery books with their presupposition that certain flavours merge with certain others. I also discover that poets and novelists from very different cultures often catch and illuminate my experience by those they describe, or that I can share wordlessly jokes or uneasinesses with other people.

The difficulties about trusting a religious tradition are more specific. In some forms of Buddhism, it is apparently thought possible for the believer to detect when he has achieved Enlightenment. Various practices are described as leading to quite specific results, and a man is invited to adopt the practices and verify the outcome within his own finite experience. There is no aspiration towards the transcendent. In most cases, however, it is almost a matter of definition that the reality which the religious believer encounters can hardly be grasped or expressed and it is doubtful if even Buddhism is a true exception. Accounts which are passed on are therefore already to some extent a distortion of the situation, for instance, when religious language uses the image of talking to or hearing an individual being. If after that, generations imagine themselves into situations where they actually are talking to an individual, others may well find they can no longer trust reports of such experiences.

The contexts in which trusting someone might reasonably influence one's tendency to believe are therefore fairly immediate

[1] Solipsism is the technical name given to the position of scepticism about the reality of the external world or other people.

41

ones. They are situations where one can know someone well enough to probe fairly thoroughly, or where it is clear how he stands in relation to the language he uses. In addition, of course, they are situations where the person is trustworthy, has the sort of integrity which sustains belief.

Where one has no direct access to such intimate grounds for belief, religious traditions sometimes appeal to authority. Crudely, this argument is expressed in the old revivalist song:

> It was good enough for Moses,
> It's good enough for me.

More subtly, it is the suggestion that certain people or writings have some kind of guaranteed insight, which vindicates the beliefs they express.

In Christianity, the most popular candidates have been the Church (because of the alleged continuity from the time of the apostles who knew Jesus) and the Scriptures (because of their assumed inspiration by the Holy Spirit).

Clearly, authority is sometimes an argument for belief. If a report of an assassination is given on the B.B.C. news, it is probably true. If a parchment is handed to an undergraduate saying that the University confers on him the degree of B.A., it is reasonable to believe that he is a B.A. The authority of these institutions' pronouncements is closely linked to their credentials. In the former case, the B.B.C. could no longer be taken as authoritative if its news reports were consistently inaccurate and badly researched. University degrees could not be plausibly conferred unless the control of graduation procedures was carefully supervised.

The main point of all this is that authorities have to be able to prove their case. We no longer accept 'because Aristotle says so' as a reason for believing something, as the Middle Ages did. Even Aristotle must justify himself.

So with religious authorities. Suppose we establish that Apostolic Tradition is fairly continuous right back to Jesus. What does continuity prove? Are eye witnesses any more protected from misunderstanding than other men? Can nearness to events not often mean one gets them out of perspective? Or suppose we find passages in Scripture claiming authority. Does the making

42

of a claim establish its correctness? If so, why is history so littered with discarded authorities who have claimed to know things? Given what is now clear about the way the Bible was compiled, or about the character of individual documents, can we treat its statements as hermetically sealed off from human error?

As a matter of psychology, then, people may appeal to authority or to the trust they have in people as a defence of their belief. These will only be effective *rational* defences, however, if they can also show *why* an authority is authoritative or *how* the people in question are trustworthy. Similarly, the effects or results of belief may persuade people to give it a try, but they cannot, no matter how impressive, prove that what is believed is true.

DISCUSSION QUESTIONS

How far do you think faith is handicapped or helped if it is not rationally provable?

Do you think it is sometimes moral and sometimes immoral to believe what cannot be proved? How would you discriminate if you think belief beyond the evidence is only *sometimes* irresponsible?

FOR FURTHER READING

W. James, *The Varieties of Religious Experience*, Chapter 3. Fontana.

P. Berger, *A Rumour of Angels*. Allen Lane.

5

CHOOSING AND BELIEVING

> The voice of an older man began to question him, and Nunez found himself trying to explain the great world out of which he had fallen, and the sky and the mountains and sight and such like marvels to those elders who sat in darkness in the Country of the Blind. And they would believe and understand nothing whatever he told them.
>
> H. G. WELLS *The Country of the Blind*

'If you refuse to believe me, I can only warn you that you'll regret it.' 'He should be ashamed of himself, a man of his education believing such things.' 'I know I shouldn't believe there's no hope, but I do.' 'They won't believe I mean it.' 'We've decided to give you the benefit of the doubt.'

All these natural-sounding sentences imply something like the conviction that people have a responsible choice about their beliefs. This seems to be frequently assumed in religious contexts too, from the appeals considered in the last chapter to the exhortations of street preachers that their hearers should repent and believe. Unbelief has frequently been classified as a sin, where 'sin' is understood as involving moral failure, and a great deal of well-established usage seems to support the suggestion that you can choose what you believe.

Suppose, on the other hand, that I invite you to believe that you are at present asleep. You are having a sophisticated dream in which you realize that you *are* dreaming, or even wonder if you are. But you are. The dream is very convincing because the cohesion of elements in it is strong; you seem to be hearing, seeing and touching a world as ordered as the waking world. Nevertheless you fell asleep during the reading of the last paragraph. You are now dreaming. In a few moments a door will bang, or your head will jerk, or your arm slip off the chair

44

and you will wake up and find that half-an-hour has gone by since you started this chapter.

Do you believe it? Does trying help? Or do you protest that no amount of effort is relevant to the matter? You *cannot help* believing that you are at this moment fully conscious, and though you may be quite liable to fall asleep, you are unable to believe you are likely to fall awake and find this to be a dream. There is no choice involved.

Certainly that seems to be the case about so many immediate beliefs that it appears odd even to speak of 'believing' these things at all. We might be tempted to answer, like Dr Johnson when asked if he believed in the freedom of the will, 'Sir, we *know* our will is free, and *there's* an end on't'.

Of course one could contrive situations which would make even these basic convictions rock. Suppose your friends decided to play a practical joke on you by *acting* as if you were asleep. They talked in hushed tones, saying things like, 'Sshh, don't wake him'. They made no response to things you said, or movements you made, and went about with no sign that they regarded you as a conscious person in the room. Further, they were skilled enough not to giggle, or to look conspiratorial, but just to go about their other business.

That might really undermine your confidence that you were not asleep. You might slide from, 'I know I'm awake' to 'I'm sure I'm awake' to 'I think I'm awake', or even say to yourself, 'What am I to believe?'. Such challenges are rarely put, however, to the vast majority of our 'working convictions' about the world, colour, shape, our own bodies, our own sensations, and even other people's. One has to be intellectually hijacked by a professional philosopher to go around worried that much of one's supposed knowledge is 'only' belief.

What such imaginable challenges establish is that theoretical alternatives are possible. As Tom Stoppard says in his play *Jumpers*, 'all the observable phenomena associated with the train leaving Paddington could equally well be accounted for by Paddington leaving the train'.

That does not mean that people have *in fact* the option of believing the alternative. If for instance they are unaware of the option they cannot possibly accept or deny it.

We can however push the question of responsibility further

back. How far are people responsible for what they are aware of, or unaware of? Let us consider some examples.

In H. G. Wells' story quoted above, Nunez arrives by chance in a valley cut off for fourteen generations from the outside world. In the community there, everyone is blind, and he alone can see. The names for everything connected with sight have faded out of use, so the people's vocabulary no longer contains words like 'see', 'blind', 'darkness', and they understand none of the activities which depend on such things. Nunez cannot convince them by his visual competence that he is abler than they, for they have no scale by which to measure 'visual competence'. Indeed their other senses are so developed, their days so ordered, their village so suited to their condition, that Nunez is the one who appears clumsy and incompetent. They do not believe him when he tells them what the world looks like, and regard him as either impious or imbecile.

Hearing the plot, one might be tempted to say, 'But, of course, blind men can't be expected to believe in those circumstances. They can have no concept of the world of sight'. The story however hints that there is a kind of perversity in their refusal to listen to Nunez, a resistance of will as well as a limit of imagination. It is implied that if they had given him a sympathetic hearing, he *might* have been able to persuade them to believe that there was a world where people saw.

Situations where it becomes most plausible to suggest that people *choose* to believe things are typically those where they have some stake in the belief. For the inhabitants of the Country of the Blind, the whole world would have fallen apart if they had been convinced that they were wrong. This may be the case with many of the beliefs people hold in such spheres as politics or ethics, where a change in belief would mean a change in practice or attitudes, or where it involves a judgement on their own past.

Suppose, for instance, that someone believes public schools should be compulsorily abolished. He is convinced that they are dens of privilege and bastions of obsolete values, damaging to their members and to society at large. This complex belief involves several judgements about facts, and, at least in principle, the facts could be ascertained. One could, that is, by diligent and scrupulous enquiry find out: what the average income of

46

parents of pupils at such schools is, what the examination success rates are, what future careers pupils take up, what percentage of pupils go to Oxbridge, what percentage of these pupils are academically less able than pupils from other schools who don't get places. One could also establish what the political allegiance of former pupils is, how many go into politics, how many former public school pupils send *their* sons to public schools, how many remember hating their schooldays, how many show signs of severe personality disturbance and how many gain outstanding public distinction.

Actually, choices one makes may affect one's judgement even of such apparently straightforward matters of fact. The papers one chooses to read, the people whose company one enjoys may in time limit or expand one's access to the data. In that sense one may be responsible for one's beliefs, in that they might have been liable to be different had one made different choices earlier.

Secondly, even if the basic data are forthcoming, the facts could be construed in different ways. If there were a statistically significant correlation between public school attendance and personality disturbances, this need not prove that the latter was *because* of the former. There might be two independent facts coinciding: that more of the aristocracy than anyone else can afford public schools and that the aristocracy, like thoroughbred horses, are so finely tuned as to be particularly vulnerable to psychiatric disorder.

Or suppose it were established that more public school pupils with poor 'A' levels got into Oxbridge than people with the same results from elsewhere. That might mean that a sinister liaison operated between two traditions of privilege or it might indicate Oxbridge reluctance to create a sheer intellectual meritocracy and be construed as an attempt to tone down the rampant scholarship of grocers' sons from grammar schools with smatterings of relatively brainless aristocratic culture.

The 'real facts' here would be even harder to ascertain, but with enough subtlety, one might, theoretically, manage. It would take one into much wider areas of investigation to cover all the relevant variables and guarantee adequate control tests. How many non-public school aristocrats have nervous disorders, and how many public school non-aristocrats do? How many of

47

the academically poorer freshmen have had family connections in the same college? Are non-intellectual types from other cultural backgrounds admitted too? What sorts of contacts are there between schools and colleges?

In concrete situations, of course, it can be extraordinarily hard to 'get at the facts'. Even the most cynical about the ways of the world, however, can recognize the theoretical difference between a prejudiced survey and an open one. Again, choices made earlier may well affect the actual openness to the truth which anyone can achieve at a given stage, but, hopefully, if someone aims to 'get at the facts', it is possible, on that level, for him to believe responsibly.

The most crucial area of debate though is still ahead. Suppose agreement or disagreement is reached about these facts. There is still a whole host of presuppositions to be explored, a whole spectrum of evaluative stances.

One person believes that the nature of a University is to be a centre of excellence, another that it should be a democratic institution of higher education for all who want it. Some believe that having an income of over £10,000 a year is immoral, others are convinced that it is a mark of commendable use of talents. Some see equality as a pernicious or Utopian myth, others as a desirable, if distant, horizon of their endeavour. Even among those who agree in having negative beliefs on the value of public schools, there are disagreements in other respects. Should one hope that such élitist establishments will wither away in time, or does one need to campaign actively for their closure? Would the social benefits in closing them be an overriding good, even if it involved the infringement of minority liberty of choice? If so, would abolition be more like banning heroin in spite of the protests of addicts, or more like banning the Hari Krishna movement against the will of its devotees?

Most answers to these questions will also express beliefs, no less than people's convictions about the facts. Even if, desirably, beliefs about *facts* are constrained by the evidence, does one not choose one's values? Is this the area where belief is a matter of choice?

There are certainly some situations where what someone believes is virtually identical with what he commits himself to. Imagine a certain pupil in a school who persistently refuses to work or to co-operate with any teacher. He is truculent if reproved, and contemptuous if not. No penalties or sanctions invoked have made any difference to his attitude, and no medical explanation of his behaviour can be found. Most people in the school now ignore the situation, those dealing with the boy having given it up as a bad job.

A new teacher comes and is put in the picture. In spite of this he does ask the boy things in class, and is met with insolence or studied silence. He goes on inviting him to take part in class projects, and is appalled by the disruptive effect if the boy does participate. In the end, other resentful members of the class complain, and the headmaster calls the teacher in.

'Look, Brown', he says, 'I could have understood it if you were straight from college. But you've had ten years' experience. You must have come across this kind of customer before. Haven't you?' Brown concedes the point. 'And have you ever seen your methods make a difference to that sort?' 'Not measurably', admits Brown. 'Well, why on earth do you persist with them?' 'I just believe that you have to go on treating people like people, even if they abuse that trust.' 'But you don't have any confidence that Grimsby will change his spots?' 'I don't know, sir, but I believe he must be treated as if he could.'

In this case Brown accepts the facts. He agrees that the chances of Grimsby changing are slim. He allows that his methods have no evident results. His belief, however, is in some way independent of the facts, 'against the odds'. It is a commitment to a certain stance, come what may.

Is this significantly different from the situation of the man who goes on believing that the British are more intelligent than other races, even if every neutral test suggests the contrary? In a way both are flying in the face of the facts. Brown, however, recognizes what the facts are, while the Jingoist is obliged either to deny them, or literally to contradict himself. In the latter case, the belief is allegedly factual, in the former it is primarily a matter of commitment to a policy.

Several theologians in recent years have suggested that Christian belief is more like the former than the latter. The theological witness in Chapter 3 was moving along these lines, and he is in fairly substantial (if disputedly good) company. Donald Evans, for instance, in *The Logic of Self-Involvement* spends a whole

49

book expounding a position of this sort. His particular thesis is that to believe 'the world was made by God' does not mean accepting some assertion about a supernatural event at the beginning of time. Rather it means committing oneself to operate in the world as if it were given for responsible tenure, it means accepting that 'onlook' on life.

There is a central debate in the philosophy of religion today as to the merit of this kind of account of belief. Those who view it positively see Christianity at last shaking itself free from an alien captivity. They suggest that in the last two or three hundred years, the rise of the natural sciences has so impressed people that their imagination has been brainwashed. They have assumed that all true assertions were quasi-scientific ones. And they have assumed that all scientific assertions were literal and objectively verifiable by public methods of checking. By this standard, religious dogmas have been notoriously unable to prove themselves. The significant question is whether that is so much the *worse* for religious dogma or so much the *better*. To some, at least, it seems a gain that scientific assertion should be denied the monopoly of truth. If only the theologians had never started to fight as if they were competing with scientists on how the universe was, it could, on this view, have been faithful to its origins, and not forced into apparent retreat by the new disclosures of the sciences.

On the other hand, Alasdair MacIntyre, author of *The Religious Significance of Atheism*, thinks that it is theism which is in retreat. The interest in withdrawing Christian stakes in 'what the facts are' seems to him mere loss of nerve. 'Theists are offering atheists less and less in which to disbelieve', he suggests. 'Theism thereby deprives active atheism of much of its significance and power' (p. 124). Also, by implication, it loses its *own* significance and power, and any right to claim to be *describing* the real world.

Whether or not the price of so interpreting it is too high, the more belief can be understood as commitment of some sort, the more intelligible the notion of choosing a belief becomes. That does not, of course, relieve one of the onus to give some sort of rational grounds for beliefs. A man may be insane in his choices, just as he may be in his convictions about the world. This position, however, also raises colossal problems about the continuity of the tradition. How can this interpretation of belief be squared with the Christian past?

It is fairly easy to argue that theologians have rarely thought they could speak about God in a systematic body of assertions as literally true as a chemistry textbook's account of substances (though interesting things are being suggested nowadays about the non-literalness of even scientific statements; but that's another story). Only biblical or doctrinal fundamentalists have assumed that their religious indicatives ('God spoke to Moses', 'The Logos is of One substance with the Father') correspond literally to natural or supernatural states of affairs, like descriptions of chemical reactions or the components of compounds. The majority of theologians have recognized some distance between their language and the reality about which they were trying to be articulate and have seen such claims to literal truthfulness as idolatrous.

The problem is to specify in what sense, then, religious affirmations *do* relate to the reality which concerns the believer. If they are not even *meant* as literal descriptions it is inept to judge them for failing in that capacity. But is it not rather implausible to reinterpret all religious or theological language as *merely* the expression of commitments put in an indicative or narrative form? How past theologians have assessed the status of their own language is a delicate historical question, made more difficult by the linguistic unselfconsciousness of much of the past. How it *should* be assessed (whether they got it right or not) is an ongoing contemporary discussion which must be conducted outside the boundaries of this book, though the debate about belief and the debate about language are inseparable.[1]

We have not yet completely opened up the question of choice and belief, far less explored its intricacies. It is clear that choice may play a part in the evidence one will listen to where beliefs are about matters of fact. It is also obvious that *some* beliefs are really commitments to act in a certain way, or convictions that such actions are desirable.

Some theologians talk as if there were still a third possibility,

[1] For further discussion of this and related points, see Peter Donovan, *Religious Language*, No. 2 in the 'Issues in Religious Studies' series. Sheldon Press.

namely the choice to believe that something is the case in the absence of sufficient evidence.

This seems to be the position which John Hick adopts in several of his books. Concisely, he argues as follows. In the world as we have it, God is not clearly manifest. If he were, men would be so dazzled, so coerced into worship that they would have no more freedom than moths round a light. God therefore sets the world 'at a distance' from himself. The distance is not spatial or temporal but 'epistemic', that is, it is a distance of knowledge. We are not given immediate knowledge of God, and this is for our good.

Apart from his reluctance to annihilate us by the force of his immediate presence, God intends a positive good from this 'epistemic freedom'. The good is that we should follow our instinct for belief, testing it against obstacles, purging it of opportunist tendencies, responding to the hints of God which will confirm our faith if we choose to follow them up, but which will not coerce our belief if we choose to ignore or deny them.

If Hick really means it, however, when he admits that the world is only ambiguously God's, it is hard to see how 'deciding to believe' can be distinguished from 'acting as if you believed' or simply from indulging in wishful thinking. One might, of course, decide to explore, or to take a belief seriously, and that in time might lead to the discovery that one actually *could* believe—that the belief had 'become credible'. One might even invest one's longing on one side or another. Blougram challenged Gigadibs in these terms too:

> You like this Christianity or not?
> It may be false, but will you wish it true?
> Has it your vote to be so if it can?

Such a disposition to regard possibilities with delight or longing remain, however, on the level of *entertaining* the belief in question. To blur the distinction between that and actually believing would be like ignoring the difference between travelling hopefully and arriving. Nor can one abandon the distinction between acting *as if* something were true and believing *that it is*. The former is a possible policy though one not easy to square with

52

the demand for integrity of action and belief, which implies one's awareness that it may not be true or even that it is false. The latter does not allow an option of sitting loose to the question of the truth of the belief. What I believe to be true may actually be false, but I cannot simultaneously *recognize* that it is false and believe it to be true. One could, unless one had absolute principles against lying in any circumstances, think of some situations where behaving as if something were the case when it is known not to be might be justified. It would be very odd, though, to describe even such justified preferences as 'believing' even if it was to oneself that one was pretending. It would, incidentally, be even odder if such use of the term had its currency in a faith which claims any concern with truthfulness.

If belief is anything to do with choice, there is a further need to work out what count as responsible or irresponsible choices, some kind of 'ethic of believing'. That is a distinct though related issue. This chapter's main concern has been to clarify the sense in which it is even intelligible to speak of choosing in relation to belief.

It does make some kind of sense for Francis Thomson's poem to dramatize his spiritual progress as *evasion* of pursuit by the Hound of Heaven. It equally makes sense for those who have believed and stopped believing to record that they *refused* for long periods to entertain their growing doubts about a given faith. People *can* often deliberately avoid letting their belief be questioned. They can wilfully disregard evidence, or they can 'push things to the back of their minds'.

However, by the time a woman is 'refusing to believe' that her husband is unfaithful she is already entertaining the possibility that he is. If she simply *doesn't* believe it, the question of 'refusing to' doesn't arise.

One can, of course, choose to give someone the benefit of the doubt, but this is a fairly provisional and tentative kind of commitment. In the face of inconclusive evidence to the contrary one may go ahead on the assumption that, for instance, some injury was done with generous motives and not with wilful malice. For many religious people, the only response to the problem of evil is to give God the benefit of the doubt that 'it will all turn out for the best in the end', or that he knows what he is doing, or that he cares about what happens in the world.

If one already believes in God, and has a certain concept of him, 'giving him the benefit of the doubt' may be an intelligible, if religiously curious, thing to do. It is much more doubtful whether one can intelligibly 'give God the benefit of the doubt that he exists in the first place'. Or perhaps Newman's soldier who prayed, 'O God, if there be a God, save my soul, if I have a soul' was doing just that. His situation has a different tone, though not a less paradoxical character, from the cynical joke 'God does not exist, and it is prudent to pray to him from time to time'. The dilemma is that one either *presupposes* God's existence by invoking him, or is so very doubtful about it that 'invoking' seems impossibly hypocritical. The phrase 'giving the benefit of the doubt' hardly makes sense except in contexts where a person to *whom* the benefit is given can already be assumed.

One might, however, say there was some analogy between giving a person the benefit of the doubt and continuing to explore the religious possibility. In both, the stance one adopts may affect what one discovers. People open up only to certain approaches, as in fairy tales frogs turn into princes only when treated with love. There is no neutral public way of establishing in advance that they are really princes in disguise. It may be that the ultimate 'character' of reality can be similarly appreciated only from certain positions. There are, of course, further theological problems about traditional God-talk if his effective disclosure is so dependent on human choices. Nevertheless, the notion is intelligible. Of course, if the would-be believer is *wrong* to give the world the benefit of the doubt that it is God's, the risk is not of being let down by a person. It is rather a risk of being cosmically foolish, as Vladimir and Estragon may be in Beckett's *Waiting for Godot*. In the last resort, though, even this is only *willingness* to believe, openness to the *possibility* of faith. That could be called 'belief' only by courtesy, though it may be a courtesy extended by evangelical tradition. 'Lord, I believe; help thou mine unbelief' suggests something of the sort. Pascal's other famous saying puts into God's mouth the words, 'Be comforted. You would not be seeking me if you had not found me'. If that is well imagined, the implication seems to be that 'exploring' may be a mode of relating to God, a form of believing, in which the believer believes without knowing it.

The courtesy, however, cannot be assumed or exploited, and it would be Pickwickian to recommend that 'belief' should be so redefined. Quite clearly for some purposes one wishes to distinguish between even committed exploration and achieved belief. If the distinction is irrelevant from the point of view of relatedness to God, that is a theological insight which even believers find highly controversial. Asserting that one can believe by a certain kind of doubting is a paradox warranted, if at all, only by the sort of context where people dare to renounce prose for poetry.

If the achievement of religious belief in some way depends *on* the decision to explore it, then choice has some indirect bearing on it. If, however, to believe something is *to be convinced* that it is the case, one can't actually be convinced just by choosing. Indeed, as we shall see in the next chapter, it is sometimes argued that 'being convinced' is not *at all* a matter of one's decisions, but a situation to which choice is as irrelevant as it is to being hungry.

DISCUSSION QUESTIONS

Do your convictions about religion seem to you to be chosen or not? Could you change them by deciding to? Do you think it is ever appropriate to blame people for their religious beliefs or lack of them?

If someone said he was willing to believe, but couldn't, what would you tell him to do?

FOR FURTHER READING

S. Kierkegaard, *Fear and Trembling* Collected Works III p. 100ff (on the Knight of Faith). Princeton University Press.

6

EXPLANATIONS OF BELIEF

I knew a witty physician who found the creed in the biliary duct, and used to affirm that if there was disease in the liver, the man became a Calvinist, and if that organ was sound, he became a Uniarian.   EMMERSON *Essays*

So far, the discussion has been conducted as if the only question about belief were questions about how to *justify* believing, as if any answer to the question 'Why believe?' will be a *reason* supporting the belief or the believing.

There are, however, other kinds of questions and answers. If someone is asked 'Why do you limp?' he isn't usually being asked to *justify* limping, he is being asked to *explain* his lameness.

Some things can be explained when no question of justifying them arises, for instance many phenomena in the natural world. 'Why does the sun rise in the East and set in the West?' 'Why does the stomach not digest itself as well as its contents?' 'Why do trees wither in autumn?'

People can sometimes be asked, and can answer, questions about themselves by giving that sort of explanation: 'Why do you limp?' 'I had an accident when I was a child.' 'Why are you laughing?' 'It's a nervous tic I get when I'm under strain.' 'Why do you go to Margate for your holidays?' 'Oh, my father just refuses to go anywhere else.'

Some questions, depending on the context, may invite either an explaining answer or a justifying one, and some replies may serve both to explain and to justify. The person who goes to Margate may by his answer be making it clear that he has no choice in the matter. In that case he is not even trying to justify Margate as a holiday destination, he is explaining why he goes.

It's almost something that happens to him rather than something he does. If, on the other hand he answers 'Well, we live in a tiny wee place, and it makes a nice change to see a bit of life' or 'All my old friends live there and I like to visit them every year', these are ways of justifying the choice, and imply accepted responsibility for the action.

Technical philosophical discussions sometimes keep the word 'reason' for the justifying sort of answer, and 'explanation' for the ones where no question of justification arises. This may simplify discussion, but it hardly reflects the way in which explanation and justification may slide into one another, or the actual practice of ordinary speech, where people tend to use both words interchangeably.

'Oh, that explains it!' a questioner might say when told about the friends in Margate. 'So that's the reason' the response might come to the information about the limp. It would be curiously pedantic in everyday life to reject such rejoinders and insist on reversing the vocabulary. With that reservation, however, it may be some aid to clarity if we keep the term 'reason' in this discussion for *justifying* answers to 'why' questions, and 'explanations' for *non-justifying* ones.

The offering and accepting of *reasons* presupposes that people are, at least in some measure, free agents, able to respond rationally, and to give grounds for what they do. The offering of explanations assumes no such thing. Indeed it may, by implication, exclude or undermine reasons.

Suppose Mr Jones is asked why he's going home by such a roundabout route on a particular evening. He offers as his reason that he wants to hand in a birthday present to Mr Oliver, and in fact does so. His discerning colleague, however, having observed his behaviour over the last few weeks suspects that the real explanation is Jones's hope that he may bump into Miss Crispin who lives round the corner from Mr Oliver. He accepts Jones's account politely enough, but thinks to himself, 'I bet he'd have found a reason anyway. It's really that he'll take any chance to get a glimpse of Miss Crispin.'

The two accounts don't necessarily clash. Jones need not be lying. He may not even be aware himself of how often he finds perfectly good reasons for being in the area where the lady is likely to appear. From outside, though, an astute observer might isolate 'the real reason' as the attraction to Miss Crispin.

By calling it the 'real' reason he would mean that it alone would be enough to determine Jones' action, while none of the others would. In terms of motivation the other reasons are merely pretexts. The driving spring of the action is the hope of seeing her.

Reasons which are not 'the real explanation' are often called 'rationalizations', and the phenomenon has been recognized for as long as human beings have recorded one another's behaviour. Satirists in particular are quick to spot it, and people are characteristically more open to suspect it in others than in themselves.

The term itself has gained currency since the work of Freud became widely known, for he emphasized the frequency with which compulsive or neurotic desires were disguised, even from the *desirer*, by the production of alleged reasons for his action.

Freudian theories have been open to much criticism, and to increased refinement, but the impact of his work has hugely affected the self-understanding of Western Europe. There was a time when people would have been confident that the way to self-knowledge was through introspection—the scrutiny of one's own consciousness. Freud's successes in psychoanalysis suggested rather that people could be far more disguised from themselves than even honest self-scrutiny *could* recognize. He often found that he reached the centre of people's problems by ignoring what they said were their reasons for doing things. Instead he concentrated on factors which they had never connected with their behaviour—dreams, superstitious practices, slips of the tongue and so on. Often, when these things were explored and pursued, rather than the rational accounts patients would have given of their own behaviour, the illness was dramatically cured.

All this has made us more aware that people may do a thing, believing they do it for some reason or other, but in fact driven by needs in themselves which they had not acknowledged. Indeed, if Freud was right, these needs could not possibly be recognized by the agent, since they belong to the life of the *sub*conscious, by definition hidden from our consciousness.

Freud himself was convinced that religious belief was, like neurotic behaviour, a way of allowing the subconscious to cope with its unsolved problems. He suggested different accounts of this in various writings. One was that belief in God was the

58

projection of an omnipotent father, a way of handling the love and fear that were found in the child's response to his own father Another suggested that the idea of Providence was in the wish-fulfilment of man's need, in his weakness, to feel safe from the caprices of nature and life. Or again, it could be that the notion of a cosmic lawgiver was an externalized form of taboos on unlimited pleasure-seeking forced on children's instinctual life by society.

At any rate, one central point was repeated: religious belief is a kind of unhealthiness of the subconscious. If people could be healed psychologically they would stop believing. What they now offer as genuine reasons for belief would then dissolve and evaporate. While in the past it was a tolerable way of coping with areas of unresolved anxiety, man is now in a position to find better, more rational ways of doing that within his human community. The illusion of religous belief is no longer conducive to individual or social welfare.

Many critics have rejected Freud's specific argument as unproven or inconsistent. They point out the impossibility of checking some of his assertions. They argue, too, that he chose particularly unsophisticated forms of belief to undermine. At the same time, they give the impression of being worried. The Freudian account of belief somehow gets under their skin, and its general thrust, if not its detail, appears menacing.

We cannot here go into all the details of this fascinating debate, but one or two points must be noted.

It is hard to deny, either from commonsense experience or from psychological research that people sometimes do things giving what they believe to be reasons, when quite different factors are the *real* explanation. It does not follow, however, that *whenever* anyone gives a reason for anything he is really rationalizing. Not even Freud claimed that, and in many of his writings he offers reasoned arguments for or against believing things or acting in certain ways. Any generalization that *all* beliefs are sufficiently explained on psychological grounds sturdily saws off the branch on which *that* belief is blossoming.

In addition, as people frequently point out, Freud's encounters with religious belief were mainly in the context of neurotic patients. What might emerge, even as valid generalization, about the religious belief of neurotics need no more hold for all religious belief than what is common among the state of kidneys in a kidney unit will show about the condition of an average British kidney. Of course it would be hard to prove conclusively that there *aren't* subconscious determinants of all religious belief, but it is fairly clear that not all religious believers are neurotic by any independent standard of neurosis. Such experiments as have been done in this area suggest that such a thesis could only be maintained by begging the question it set out to answer. If 'All religious belief is neurotic' is supposed to be an empirical claim, its defenders must produce enough evidence to make it convincing. If it then turns out that the 'evidence' they produce is merely a *definition* that 'All religious belief is neurotic' they are begging the question, not proving anything about the real character of religious belief. It is like a man arguing that 'All modern art is formless', whose response when invited to consider the form of this or that work is, 'But I don't need to look. If it's modern it's bound to be formless.'

Even if it were established that religious belief emerges out of some kind of human need, and withers when the need disappears, would that prove that the belief were false? Suppose it were true that God existed and had made man. Would it not then be natural if man felt some kind of incompleteness, the kind of itch for God which theologians have sometimes used as an argument for his existence? It is not, of course, a very good argument. People can be thirsty even if there is nothing for them to drink. On the other hand, the fact that they dream of water when they thirst doesn't prove, or even confirm, that there is no such substance.

It may be that Voltaire was right to suggest that if God did not exist, it would be necessary to invent him. But that does not prove of itself that he doesn't exist. It merely suggests that he *needn't* in order for religious belief to arise. The fact that any number or type of people believe in God is of itself neither proof nor disproof of his existence. Nor is the fact that any number or type disbelieve in him. To make theological or atheistic capital out of such figures requires a good deal more argument.

It is, in any case, doubtful if many generalizations can be made about personality types of religious believers. What research has been done on the question with empirical testing suggests some link between religious belief and authoritarian personalities. This, however, emerged as less true of very strongly committed religious believers than of those with fairly peripheral involvement. Of course one can find people who seem to use religion as a kind of fantasy wish-fulfilment; but there are others in whom it creates such restlessness and dissatisfaction with the *status quo* that they would have been much more comfortable without it. Some believers are quietist, some are activist, some love life, some hate it, some appreciate the authority which religious tradition may invoke, others respond to the freedom by which they find much of the tradition judged. Indeed the more aware one is of the range and variety of religious belief, doctrine and practice, the more inadequate any generalization becomes.

Why then the alarm which Freudian accounts of religious belief generate in many defenders of the faith? It is not that empirical causes for religious belief in general have been established. It is not even that, if they were, the beliefs would necessarily be false.

The anxiety is probably related to the hope most people have, if they raise such questions at all, that their beliefs are not only true, but that they have come to hold them by discriminating and reasonable estimates of the situation in question. What a man believes as a result of propaganda or hypnotism may in fact be true, but *his* belief is not a matter of free rational consideration. What Freud seems to threaten is not the possible truth of this or that belief but confidence that we are capable of appraising the truth. The old religious nightmare of predestination thus reappears in a new guise. Not unseen decrees of providence, but subconscious fears and desires dictate what will appear to me as true. I may reassure myself that what I believe can survive rational scrutiny, but it may be that if I found myself faced with beliefs contradicting what I *needed* to believe, I would simply cook the intellectual books. This would not be an act of deliberate dishonesty; it would be a natural process, like scar tissue forming over a wound. My mind would be the prisoner of my emotional needs, but I could never know it, since it is part of the warders' subtlety that they encourage every illusion of intellectual freedom.

Scepticism about rationality as such would obviously undermine confidence about the reasonableness of believing anything.

61

Religious men would have no more to lose than atheists. A more specific challenge suggests that the scepticism applies mainly to those areas of belief where emotions are strongly involved. Here religion would obviously be a strong candidate for suspicion, though some brands of atheism show more ferocious emotional involvement than many affirmations of religious belief.

Not only may a Freudian explanation challenge those who hope their belief is free and rational, it may threaten those who believe it to be a direct, supernatural gift from God. There are great difficulties for any theologian trying to give an account of 'grace'. How does God's initiative relate to human freedom or the world's regularities? Does he move molecules around, or invade hormones, or stimulate brain cells? Or is his 'activity' a more complex relation to what is going on in wholly natural processes? Theologians taking the latter line have problems explicating the 'more complex relation', but can remain unworried by increases in psychological knowledge. Those who insist that God's action is an independent and sufficient cause of belief must feel more under pressure. Just as in the late 1890s some found it a straight fight between Darwin and God, so on this issue Freud seems to some to offer a theory of the origin of religious belief directly competing with God as its explanation.

When people doubt their own rationality in believing, it is natural for them to go on to wonder if *what* they believe is true. Freud's account of how people come to believe does not, however, by itself disprove anything. In his writings he himself combines his account of believing with reasoned arguments against the content of religious belief. The second strand involves the sort of discussion undertaken earlier in this book. Questions of truth and falsity, then, cannot be reduced to questions of psychology. On the other hand, awareness of psychological possibilities might make us more modest in our claims to know the truth. But modesty is a different thing from total loss of nerve. Recognition that I am liable to cheat myself psychologically makes me more aware of how very hard it is to know or speak the truth. But very hard comes well short of impossible.

We have taken up the Freudian account in some detail, as typical of a whole approach to belief, the general type being called 'reductionist'. The mark of a reductionist position is the fallacy of 'nothing-but'. Belief is *nothing but* the result of your toilet training. A belief system is *nothing but* a function of economic structures, of social organization, of cultural thought patterns, of climate. Because of that it can be *explained away* as a serious candidate for truth.

One difficulty about reductionist accounts is that they swallow each other, but rarely swallow themselves. A Marxist will accuse a Freudian of being a victim of class-structures in the formation of his belief, while the Freudian explains the Marxist's convictions by psychoanalysing him. A social anthropologist suggests that one African tribe is polytheistic because it is constitutionally monarchic, and another is monotheistic because it is republican. He does not, however, preface his book with the concession: 'The convictions of this work are explained by the fact that the author lives in a liberal democracy', and he probably hopes that the truth of his belief will be persuasive across cultural boundaries.

At the same time, the extravagance of some reductionist claims should not give us any delusions of grandeur about the autonomy of our beliefs. Obviously a man's culture, social background, infantile neuroses, glands, digestion are liable to affect his beliefs, as are the books he reads, the friends he has, the things which happen to him. That is to say, a person is not a belief-selecting vacuum, an isolated rational will. His past and his present environment go into the making of him, and thus in the making, he judges what seems true and what false.

The proper weight which should be given to any alleged explanation of belief cannot be decided in advance. It depends on the quality of evidence backing the account. Freud is finally unconvincing, because his account in the end seems to fit only highly selected data, not because there *couldn't* be a link between religion and neurosis.

So, if one was examining, say, a Marxist account of religious belief, one would have to look at how religious belief and class are related. Is it empirically true that belief can be found only among the alienated, exploited poor? If not, can any account of it as merely the opium of the oppressed be substantiated? What is the role of the institutional church in the economic life of the people? Is it a stimulus towards radical social change, or an anchor of the *status quo*? Does it consist mainly of one social class? Is its *power* mainly in the hands of one social class? Does it invariably encourage passivity about politics among its members? How individualist are its central concepts of salvation or ethics? Is there any relation between its words about 'peace', 'justice', 'brotherhood' and its practice, or are these terms the hypocritical tribute of a self-centred life style, a sedative given intravenously from baptism to those in the pews?

Only detailed and scrupulous examination could confirm or negate the Marxist thesis. If, however, the production of politically radical Christians or revolutionary bishops is not allowed to count against the thesis, we have a parallel with the Freudian refusal to allow some believers to count against the view that religion is a neurosis. The thesis has now become a dogma, a *prejudging* of the issue.

External factors may certainly limit the range of options there are for people. A man who has been so culturally restricted that he has never met anyone but Plymouth Brethren, not even in books, cannot become a Buddhist. A child whose father has kicked him around from infancy cannot respond to the word 'father' with positive emotion. But such instances approach pathological imprisonment. Is it naïve to hope that people are not normally in such a condition? Can education be trusted to beat whatever indoctrinating systems people are exposed to? Can it offer the self-knowledge which allows people to transcend their conditioning? Can cultural interchange break down the stranglehold of any one set of beliefs? Or does education just replace one form of indoctrination by another, cultural exchange simply tinker with the programme which has been implanted?

In the last chapter, the difficulties about saying we choose our beliefs were explored. From this one we can perhaps see a more significant sense in which freedom of belief can be affirmed. We need not be starry-eyed about the present success of any given institution in doing the job. But so long as we find it *possible* that people can be helped to transcend their conditioning, we need not despair about belief being a by-product of impersonal factors.

Such transcendence need not mean the rejection of past beliefs, but it would allow for that possibility. A Christian might

64

become aware that he had so far taken his belief on trust from
parents or family. He might then start to talk to humanists and
explore their objections. He would read some theological discussions. He might spend some time in a country where another
faith was practised. At the end of all that, he might still remain
Christian or he might not. If he didn't change, one might hope
that his belief was more free than previously (though it could
be that he was just terribly well-conditioned before). If he did
change, one might hope that his belief was more free than before
(though it could be that he was just terribly susceptible to
reconditioning).

The analysis of what 'freedom' means in a world where
people are constantly open to external influence is a major
philosophical and theological issue. Detailed discussions are
numerous, and in this essay it is simply being assumed that even
if freedom is a relative term, it does not mean nothing.
Reductionist accounts all suggest that the occurrence of religious
belief can be sufficiently explained without any reference to
freedom in a human being. It, like him, is a product of
determinate and determining factors. Such accounts must be
given serious consideration, for they are often related to observable connections between people's conditioning and their beliefs.
When, however, they become dogmas, against which no conceivable evidence is allowed to count, the time seems ripe for
protest.

DISCUSSION QUESTIONS

Do you think any of your beliefs is likely to be true if it can be
explained why you hold it?

Which field of would-be explanation do you find the most
menacing one for religious belief?

What would have to be true for you to say that religious belief
had been successfully explained *away*?

FOR FURTHER READING

S. Freud, *The Future of an Illusion*. Hogarth Press.
L. Feuerbach, *The Essence of Christianity*, Chapter 1, § 2
'The Essence of Religion Considered Generally' (Harper Torch-
books) pp. 12-14.

7

BELIEF AND ACTION

No, no, no! I don't believe anything. Don't you see—I am
very busy with matters of consequence!
 St Exupery *The Little Prince*

But if he does really think that there is no distinction between
virtue and vice, why, Sir, when he leaves our house let us
count our spoons.   Boswell's *Life of Johnson*

If a man declares that he believes in socialism while living in
luxury, sending his children to private schools and investing
heavily in the private sector, one begins to wonder what he
means. If there were simply one area in which his action
seemed inconsistent with his declared convictions, one might
just assume that in this respect he had been untrue to his
beliefs—if, say, his wife had nagged him, against his better
judgement, into sending their children to private schools. If,
however, he seemed to observe *no* socialist principles in his
own practice, one wouldn't merely suspect him of being untrue
to his beliefs. One would suspect him of not having them.

The reason for this is that believing things has a bearing on
how one behaves. Beliefs have practical implications. If you
believe that ghosts don't exist, you will behave differently towards someone who reports having seen one than a man who
is convinced that they do. If you believe that the Bank of
England is likely to collapse next month, you will be unlikely
to keep your money in it.

At first sight it might seem that the actions implied by any
given belief could be quite easily specified. If I believe, for
example, that there is a snake in the next room, there is an
obvious limit to the behaviour congruous with such a belief.
I may shut myself in the room I'm in, blocking up all spaces

under the door and the ventilator shafts. I may risk making a dash for the 'phone or for the front door. I may even, if very foolhardy, go into the room armed with a poker and a shotgun.

If, however, I saunter nonchalantly in to do the dusting, with never a wary glance, it becomes highly implausible that I believe it. There may, of course, be exceptional circumstances. I may be an expert on snakes, and know this one to be quite harmless. Or as well as believing the snake is there, I may believe the promises of the doubtful ending of Mark's gospel about snake-handling. Or my son might be in there, and my concern for his safety outweigh my fear (though then I wouldn't be nonchalant). But one might say that there was a 'standard range' of behaviour compatible with any given belief, other things being equal.

It is easier to recognize the character of this connection between belief and action than to define it. If I say that John is a bachelor, and that his wife is charming, one could only assume that I don't *understand* the sentence 'John is a bachelor'. I'd be making a mistake in logic, failing to understand that 'being a bachelor' logically entails not having a wife. But if I say, 'I believe there's a snake in the next room', and then casually go into it, my action 'contradicts' my belief in rather a different way. Taking the risk of being bitten by a snake *is* logically compatible with believing a snake is in the room. It's just a highly eccentric and, by most standards, unintelligible response to the situation. 'You *can't* believe there's a snake and just go in like that' is a different sort of objection from 'You *can't* believe he's a bachelor and tell us you met his wife'.

Still, even if such discrepancies between belief and behaviour are not in the strictest *logical* sense 'self-contradictions', they may strike people as *practical* self-contradictions. That judgement, however, depends on certain assumptions which may be open to challenge. You doubt if I really believe there's a snake in the room because most people's response to such a situation would be fear and caution. But human beings *are* capable of untypical, surprising and inconsistent reactions in most situations. Many people, apparently, believe that smoking causes lung cancer, but don't stop smoking. This decision need not, surely, be interpreted as their denial or doubt of the link between smoking and cancer. It may just be that they haven't really thought what cancer is like. Or that they are prepared to take a risk on being one of the lucky ones. Or that, whatever the outcome, they find smoking too pleasant to give up. Or that they genuinely wish they could give it up but so far haven't managed it. Of course it *may* be the case that a man who says he believes the connection but goes on smoking doesn't really believe it, but it *need* not be. Many other explanations are possible.

What seems to be true is that people can believe things on many different levels. Some beliefs, while quite genuine, are too remote and superficial to touch any springs of action. My belief that the Amazon is 4,000 miles long is quite firm, but it has no effect whatsoever on my present existence. Similarly my conviction that half the world is starving is quite firm, but not enough in the foreground or the depth of my awareness to unsettle my three-meals-a-day routine.

It is a problem of definition, of semantics, whether one is going to restrict the use of the word 'belief' only to those convictions which a man holds so passionately that they *do* move him to action. There is an understandable scorn in the person devotedly campaigning about world hunger who finds his well-fed, untroubled audience saying, 'Yes, yes, we believe you, it's a terrible problem!' His reaction is likely to be that they don't really believe at all, either in the sense that they are hypocrites, or in the sense that they are too imaginatively and emotionally lethargic to know what 'believing' it means.

He would, however, if pressed, probably concede that his audience could be said to 'believe' him in a more minimal sense. They do not think he is lying. They know the facts put out by Oxfam. They have seen television pictures of famine relief. They accept the statistics as authoritative. They could explain to someone else what the situation is, and describe it accurately. His denial that they believe at all is a way of saying that such belief isn't worthy of the name, doesn't deserve the same title as the involved commitment of those who are acting on their belief. He insists on restricting the word to things believed 'in the bones' as well as 'in the head'. Intellectual assent is not a sufficient qualification.

It is important to recognize this dispute when one asks what action is congruous or incompatible with religious belief. The occasional opinion polls taken by Sunday papers on religious belief in Britain tend to show amazingly positive results: 85 per cent 'believe in God'; 65 per cent 'believe in some kind of after-life'. Yet very few pray regularly, or go to church, or have a life-style in any way different from the one they would have if they said 'no' to the questionnaire.

It would take delicate research to understand this situation. Do people say 'Yes' because they never think about it, and 'No' seems too strong a negative? Or because they feel the young man at the door wants them to say, Yes? Or because of a vague residual conviction that to believe in God is to be on the side of decency and order? Do they, perhaps, find the affirmation a way of signalling some conviction that is important for them, for instance that 'Nothing comes to folk that isn't meant for them', or that 'People aren't tested beyond their strength' or that 'You've just got to keep going, whatever happens'?

Professional philosophers or theologians might find these absurd or inadequate paraphrases of 'I believe that God exists', but they may in fact come closer to what people *intend* to articulate when asked if they believe than the most orthodox expositions of the Creed. The 'appropriate' action can then be judged only in the light of the assertion being made. If people's convictions are of the sort specified above, the congruous action may simply be modestly living through whatever ups and downs one meets. Instead of cutting their throats, or whining, or going sour, they accept their days and the people in their expanse of world, and go on planting potatoes or washing socks or watching their families grow away from them.

Much of the abuse heaped by the conscientiously religious on the heads of those who pay 'lip-service' to belief seems to me insensitive to such possibilities as these. One man judges that another man's action, or lack of it, is incompatible with 'belief in God' because in fact they both mean quite different things by 'belief in God'. The phrase has almost, for better or worse, got out of hand. Its actual usage seems to me far more varied than any sociologist has yet documented.

Various groups, of course, stake laims to be using the words 'I believe in God' in the *proper* way, thereby intending to disqualify any other use as improper. The concern of orthodoxy to distinguish itself from various types of heterodoxy, the working out of detailed Confessions of Faith, are attempts to resist the view that 'I believe in God' can mean anything the believer chooses to make it mean. Discussing such issues involves one in basic questions about language which are not part of the remit of this book. Are words so much a matter of convention that any words can mean anything if only enough people use them that way? Or is there some more fixed point of reference by which one can judge if words are being legitimately or illegitimately used?

The question is crucial, and will affect one's attitude to the range of meanings one is prepared to admit for the affirmation 'I believe in God'. It will therefore indirectly affect one's judgements about the relation between belief and action. Realizing that, let us now consider some of the specific problems about deciding what action is congruous with religious belief.

Tom Smith and Bill Jones both say the Apostle's Creed every Sunday, and mean it. Tom Smith has occasional twinges of intellectual conscience over the Virgin Birth, and Bill Jones wonders sometimes about the resurrection of the body, but on the whole they mean in good faith the affirmations they make, and accept the standard interpretation they were taught as Christian orthodoxy in their confirmation classes.

Tom Smith is training to be a bomber pilot, and would like to see the return of the birch and of capital punishment, as the only way of restoring law and order in a world of evaporating moral standards. Bill Jones distributes a left-wing pacifist paper, and teaches in a free school where all conventional discipline has been abolished.

How is this situation to be accounted for? One possibility is that either Smith or Jones or both believe only with 'the top of their heads'—that they have made no attempt to integrate their belief about God into their actual living. Another possibility is that both have tried to relate belief and practice, but radically disagree about what the implications are. To Jones it seems that you can't *really* believe in the Christian God and be a bomber pilot. To Smith it seems that you can't really believe in the Christian God and identify yourself with such atheist, Marxist and anarchist forces in society as Jones's colleagues represent.

To the outsider, it may well seem that a belief which allows both Jones and Smith to judge their life-styles as congruous with it is completely vacuous. The fact that there is no agreement in the Christian Church about what behaviour is properly excluded by belief in God weakens the claim that the issue of belief is of any importance.

There can be no doubt that many people who would be doctrinally compatible bedfellows can hardly coexist on the practical level. The blessings of battleships by well-intentioned bishops seem to others clear blasphemy. Approval of homosexual law reform shown by some Christians strikes others as a betrayal of unambiguous divine prohibitions. The inertia of most church members about national or international political justice provokes the radical challenge that most so-called Christians do not really believe that in Christ all men are brothers.

Does this mean that *in fact*, there is no way of relating doctrine to any specific sort of action? And if that is so, is 'believing' a luxury, a waste of time better spent getting on with 'matters of consequence'? Should one sympathize with the view that 'It doesn't matter what a man believes, so long as he does what is right'? Is there not strong justification for the view that a Buddhist or an atheist or a Unitarian or a Trinitarian can be equally kind, vicious, flexible, guilt-ridden, socially concerned or politically indifferent?

We have obviously to recognize in the religious case, as elsewhere, that people can fail to live up to their beliefs or to be consistent with them all the time. It belongs to the hiddenness of people's lives whether their claim to belief is made in hypocritical lip-service or in real pain at their own distance from goodness. Only if one believes that faith means the instant transition of a human life from imperfection to perfection could one argue the point 'You are not perfect, therefore you do not really believe'.

On the other hand, most Christians would probably be alarmed by the suggestion that one can believe and do *anything*, like Hogg's *Justified Sinner* whose conviction of salvation led him to feel free to indulge in the most outrageous immoralities. 'Feeling free to do anything' would certainly lead to a radically different life-style from most ideologies; but most Christians would probably be unhappy with the view that their faith

71

undermined all possibilities of moral discrimination. It is virtually an axiom at all levels of Christian belief that theology is bound to commit a believer to some morality or other.

It would, however, be much harder to find any consensus, even among thoughtful Christians, about what precise actions would be excluded by genuine and consistent belief. If one took the Gospel traditions as a starting point, one might suggest several which seemed to the evangelists excluded by real belief: being afraid; being anxious about tomorrow; refusing to forgive; calling one's brother a fool; hating one's enemies; holding on to one's life; laying up treasures on earth; giving automatic obedience to the laws of one's community; judging others.

One major difficulty is that, even if one agrees that belief P involves behaviour X as its consistent implication, it is not always easy to judge whether action Q is an *example* of behaviour X. *Is* taking out an insurance policy, or concern about one's salvation 'being anxious about tomorrow'? *Is* doing jury service or marking student examinations 'judging'? *Is* building and maintaining lunatic asylums 'calling one's brother a fool'? *Is* taking a university degree 'laying up treasures on earth'? *Is* protecting one's children from the deprivations others suffer, or valuing one's moral integrity 'holding on to one's life'?

Such questions can almost certainly not be answered by confident ethical generalizations. They belong to the area of discomfort which makes anyone of sensitivity unable to organize his existence by looking up the books. If, however, my alleged belief in God has no bearing at all on the question 'What am I to do now?', it seems to many people that I do not *really* believe in God.

The difficult question is what *kind* of bearing? Is it voluntary or necessary? One may see the absurdity of a claim to belief which goes with utter indifference about behaviour. It may be that I can believe the Amazon to be 4,000 miles long without that making the slightest difference to how I understand or organize my life, but can I really believe that God exists and let it make no difference?

There is a great deal of pressure from many contemporary theologians and philosophers of religion to make it a matter of definition that I *cannot*. To 'believe in God' is necessarily to be involved 'existentially'. To say 'I believe that God exists,

72

but the question doesn't interest me very much or affect my life' is, on such a view, a contradiction in terms as strictly as 'I believe he's a bachelor and I've met his wife'. Believing that God exists is not, logically, like believing that the Amazon is 4,000 miles long, not even like believing there's a snake in the next room, but is finding my existence open in certain directions and under certain constraints. Having my life affected is part of what it *means* to believe that God is real, whatever it may mean to believe that other things are the case.

This view makes sense of the indignation many observers feel at *claims* to religious belief made by 'practical atheists'. It accounts also for the widespread distrust of theologians discussing true belief snug in universities. The contention is not just that such people fail to act on their beliefs; it is that to have belief in God *means* to withdraw one's financial investments, abandon one's human isolationism, and get on with effective love of one's neighbour and that living in certain contexts precludes these possibilities from the start. No amount of impeccable ortho*doxy* is belief. Belief is ortho*praxis*, commitment to certain action, or at least being disposed in certain ways to one's own existence and that of everyone else.

There are various difficulties about this position, though anyone voicing them must suspect himself of rationalizing, of simply avoiding the challenge of an uncomfortable suggestion.

The first difficulty is that many people actually *use* the words 'believe in God' without understanding such essential involvement as part of their meaning. They would honestly say that God's existence *is* a matter of indifference to them. Simply to say that they are not understanding the words 'believe in God' seems an arbitrary short-circuiting of the discussion. They are understanding them differently. Not only that; a good deal of sophisticated Christian apologetic has assumed that it *was* intelligible (even if undesirable) for a man to be indifferent about God's existence. Those insisting, therefore, on an existentially relevant *meaning* of 'belief in God' need to justify themselves in the face not merely of popular misunderstanding, but of a different interpretation of belief within many theological circles.

The second difficulty is that the case for interpreting belief as necessarily affecting one's existence and action seems to weaken depending on which specific belief one considers. Suppose for the moment that one was persuaded to accept the existentialist account of what it meant to believe that God existed. Suppose one agreed that the difference between theism and atheism was *really* the difference between living in and for the world as one who found freedom and love at the root of it, or as one who did not. Could one do the same sort of analysis of the difference between unitarian and trinitarian theology? Or of the debate about whether the Spirit proceeds from the Father and the Son or from the Father alone? Or of the question whether the damnation of some men was appointed by God before the Fall or only after?

Perhaps with enough historical empathy one could reconstruct why people thought such questions mattered, and in so doing even see how the answers to them could make a difference to us today. Initially, however, one might be tempted to agree that many debates about belief do seem as remote as the notorious medieval one about how many angels could dance on the head of a pin. There is a common suspicion, it seems to me, that theologians as a class are given to fabricating theological issues to keep themselves in business. These have the fascination for some, of crossword puzzles, or of the invention of alternative geometries, but have no more connection than that with everyday lives.

My own conviction is that one has probably not *understood* a doctrinal debate until one realizes what is or was at stake existentially. People may, of course, hang on to positions whose implications they don't themselves see, merely because the positions come to them as authoritative tradition. What they directly care about may be the security of authoritative backing, even if they have no immediate interest in the intrinsic relevance of the affirmation. Then one has to push the question back to ask why different authorities have thought anything important was at stake in the debate. It seems to me that historical theology, when done with sensitivity, explores the issues in precisely that kind of way.

One is still free, obviously, to decide priorities of existential importance. A man may judge that in the present state of the world feeding the hungry is more important than anything else, full stop. He may also be sure that many actual discussions about religious belief *are* frivolous and empty scholasticism,

74

never touching the level where conclusions might make a difference to anyone. It may well seem to him that digging out even
the live options embedded in the obsolete idioms and cultural
debris of the past is a waste of good time.

It does seem to me, however, that theology only has a claim
to human attention in so far as it could affect any man's life
and practice. There may be things in the world which just happen to be true, like the fact that 'lettuce' is a Latin loan-word,
or that Ben Nevis is 4,406 feet high, or that the comma is used
more often in *Hamlet* than in *King Lear*. Such things interest
some people, and those who are interested are free to pursue
their study, while those who are not are free not to. The things
which believers believe, which are the concern of theology, are
not such things. 'Truth for truth's sake' is not a theological goal
unless 'truth' is understood as what relates to the question of
who I am.

There is, however, a way of framing the question of the
relevance of belief to action which makes it hard to give a
fair answer. In Erasmus's *Dialogues* one woman remarks to
another that the contemporary theological debate about free will
doesn't make much difference to the price of fish. If I believe in
God, it doesn't affect how I peel carrots, or whether I can sing
in tune, or even, perhaps, which party I vote for. (Though some
might say that peeling carrots with God in one's heart was a
different experience from peeling them otherwise! And some
might say one couldn't be a Christian Tory!) Nevertheless,
believing in God might be so bound up with one's own identity
that it made sense to say it affected everything one did. It
depends on how far one can atomize a situation and look at
the atoms. A woman in love may not find her carrot-peeling
specifically affected by the fact, but *she* is changed, and doesn't
cease to be changed when peeling carrots.

Of course, it becomes hard to see what content can be given
to the 'change' if everything is just the same as it was before.
That is the force of challenges to those who claim to believe,
but act just as they would if they claimed not to. 'Believing'
seems to shrivel into some kind of private mental process, or
some merely psychological piety.

If one agrees that religious belief implies some sort of action,
either as a defining component *or* as a proper concomitant, a

75

question remains about the possibility of reversing the relationship. If belief implies certain action, can one properly infer belief *from* certain action? Can belief be said to be implicit in action, or attitude? Suppose for instance that a man says he believes in hell, but lives in a way that indiscriminately affirms the value of all he meets. Or suppose he claims to believe that God accepts all men as they are, but lives a guilt-stricken existence of self-doubt. Is one entitled to read off his 'real' belief from his behaviour, to say of the former case 'He really believes that God's love embraces everyone, but his theology hasn't caught up', or of the latter 'He says God loves people as they are, but he doesn't really believe it'?

Some theologians have used the distinction between explicit and implicit belief to argue that all men, or at least most men, believe in God although they would not say such words as 'I believe in God'. Francis Bacon in the sixteenth century made the distinction between 'atheism on the lip' and 'atheism in the heart', and John Baillie, a liberal theologian of the 1930s, distinguished unbelief 'with the top of the head' from belief 'with the bottom of the heart'. Roman Catholic theology has sometimes implied a similar conviction in speaking about 'baptism of desire' among those who have no formal connection with church dogma or practice.

Can lives which show certain characteristics of openness, charity, freedom, be properly interpreted as showing 'implicit belief'? Or does such a claim merely reflect Christian theological greed, a refusal to allow any decency to be genuinely non-Christian; a concern to claim, even by definition, a religious monopoly of all virtue?

Again it seems a matter of semantic debate whether or not the word 'Christian' should be applied *only* to those who affirm explicit Christian dogmas; or only to those who practise what *should* follow from Christian dogma without themselves accepting the dogma. It is a matter of more substantial debate whether Christian doctrine does imply any specific moral injunctions or vetoes, and how one properly establishes them.

The two debates tend to be confused, and are obviously complicated by disagreements about what Christian dogma is or should be anyway. It is, however, important that the difficult issues they raise should be in the forefront of any study of religious belief. Philosophers in studies can easily discuss belief as if it were merely a matter of intellectual conviction. People in the street, however, may have only the most haphazard and inarticulate intellectual convictions, either because they are not much given to thinking, or because they pin on, like badges, words and affirmations which intellectuals sift and inspect. But any account of belief which presupposes philosophers as 'normal' believers is likely to be unconvincing outside philosophical circles. Indeed, a good deal of specifically Christian tradition invites closer identification of 'believing' with 'doing' than many professional thinkers might find comfortable.

It may therefore at least correct the impression that most philosophical discussion of belief and scepticism takes place in a political and existential vacuum if we reconsider the challenge, 'Show me what you *do*, and I will tell you what you believe'. The impatience of many 'outsiders' at the persistence of religion seems often related to this issue of belief and action; and there is a vast amount of exploration to be done if their concern is to be properly appreciated on the level of thought as well as action.

DISCUSSION QUESTIONS

Can the truth of a belief be properly judged by how its exponents behave?
Do Christians have to be more moral than other men if Christianity is to be convincingly true?

How would you understand the relationship between religion and morality?

FOR FURTHER READING

Helmut Gollwitzer, *The Rich Christians and Poor Lazarus*, Chapter 2. St Andrew Press.
John Hick, *Evil and the God of Love*, Chapter XIV. Fontana.

8

BELIEF AND FAITH

'You think those are your own hands, but they aren't. You think it's your own mind that's been working, nagging at the problem, and now sits in secret pride of having solved it. But it isn't. Any more than my mind speaks the words that are using my voice.'

Then they were silent again: and he was aware of the third with them, the angel that stood in the cold and rain, warming him at his back.   WILLIAM GOLDING *The Spire*

So far we have roamed, in our discussion, round many kinds of belief, presupposing that the fields involved—history, science, politics, aesthetics and religion—could all be used as parallel example-fodder. In the opening chapter, however, we had issued a warning. It could not be *assumed*, since many theologians actively denied the suggestion, that religious belief was just like political or aesthetic belief, but with a different subject-matter. Any such view had to be *argued*. In this chapter we must look at the pros and cons of classifying religious belief as a specimen of the general class 'beliefs'.

An uncompromising statement of theological opposition to this assumption is found in the article on 'Faith' in the *Oxford Dictionary of the Christian Church*. Here is one passage from it:

The widespread notion that the faith of a Christian believer in, say, the truth of the Incarnation (as a doctrine which cannot be proved) is of a piece with the scientist's faith in atoms and electrons reflects a conception of faith radically different from that of Christian orthodoxy. Faith, so far from being a mere readiness to go beyond the *data* of established fact where the evidence ceases (as does the scientist in the case just instanced) is held to be made effective by the immediate operation of the grace of God in the Christian soul, which carries with it complete conviction.

To decide what is 'orthodox' is not just a historical job. It involves the evaluation of different strands of the Christian tradition, and demands theological judgements. With luck and some education, people can move beyond the parochialism of Bishop Warburton who insisted, 'Orthodoxy is my doxy: heterodoxy is another man's doxy'. However theologians are so liable to be partisan that when one of them says something is 'radically different ... from Christian orthodoxy' one has to be careful.

How is one to decide fairly where to locate 'main-line belief'? Does one count heads, or mitres, or centuries? Could a historian ever justly say 'for something like eight centuries, orthodox Christianity disappeared from the face of Europe?' Or is that a contradiction in terms? Is orthodoxy what most of the people are believing most of the time? Is it what official creeds of the church say at any given time? And if you have different churches saying contradictory things, is the orthodox one the bigger one, or the older, or what?

We shall come back to the issue of one's relation to the tradition in the following chapter. For the time being however it would be a mammoth diversion to try to come at 'faith' by way of 'orthodoxy'. Instead of asking, then, whether the *Oxford Dictionary of the Christian Church* account is orthodox, we will ask whether it is *true*. That is not an easier question, but it is certainly more important, since orthodoxies are of interest anyway only in their claim to safeguard the truth.

In ordinary speech, people are likely to use the word 'faith' in rather more restricted contexts than the word 'belief'. One might have faith in one's boss or in the future of British democracy, or believe in either. One might have faith or believe that someone will come through an ordeal with flying colours. It would normally be odd, though, to say, 'I have faith that he's coming into town this morning'. One has to start imagining jilted brides fighting off pessimistic constructions of the groom's non-appearance, or condemned prisoners gasping for the arrival of free pardons. It is not a thing one says about friends likely to turn up for casual cups of coffee.

79

Even reflection on such usage might suggest that faith was at least as 'different' from belief as a monsoon is from wind. This implication seems supported by much radical activist literature where the distinction becomes hardened. 'Belief' in such circles may well be prescriptively limited to such anaemic intellectual convictions as they renounce. Where full-blooded involvement, commitment, engagement, trust come in, the word is not 'belief' but 'faith'.

Such distinctions are irrelevant to the dogma under scrutiny. Internally one could in any case demolish any exclusive distinction between 'belief in' or 'faith' and 'belief that'. As was suggested in the previous chapter, even belief that something is the case demands a certain range of congruous action, though the belief may be so unspectacular that the action is wholly inconspicuous. (One doesn't usually register the fact that people, by sitting confidently in chairs, manifestly believe that they will not collapse.) At the same time, most 'beliefs in' or faith stances can't be described without presupposing 'beliefs that'. Faith in the establishment of the classless society involves at least the belief that it is not yet achieved, and that it can be. Believing *that* some things are the case is at least a corollary of any committed involvement.

Even if one could make a case for distinguishing radically between 'belief in' and 'belief that' it would still not add up to the difference alleged in the article quoted above. Faith is not, by that understanding, a strong gust of natural belief blowing in certain directions. It is not even like the most deep and total trust or commitment a human being may have in the course of his developing involvement in the world around him.

The nub of this kind of theological challenge is its insistence that religious belief, or more specifically Christian belief/faith, can *never* emerge from such natural development only. A man doesn't choose his faith (not that that distinguishes faith from the many other convictions which we argued in chapter 5 were 'chosen' only indirectly). But in some more unspecified sense his faith is not 'his own doing' as his political convictions might be. A man's belief in other areas may be 'his' in the sense that *he* encounters evidence, considers data, concentrates on issues, appraises people, thinks, explores, wrestles. Even if, at the end of all that, it seems most natural to say 'He *finds himself* believing', his position is a result of his active and passive engagement, intellectually and emotionally, in his world.

On the 'orthodox' view however, faith, unlike all other belief, is never generated in such a way. A man may diligently enquire, with all his powers of rational and sympathetic interest. He may have the same world 'to go on' as the believer has. He will not however arrive at any conviction unless grace operates, inspiring him to belief. Whether faith involves assent to such doctrines as the existence and trinitarian character of God, the incarnation and the resurrection, or whether it means active trust in and devotion to God or Jesus is a secondary issue. The primary point, on this view, is that supernatural conversion is required.

Before one attempts any critical assessment of this position, one must try to specify further what is being claimed. Is it that the content of the faith is intrinsically rational, but is bound to seem irrational to the unconverted? Or is it that faith is not rational, but that the converted man can respond positively to the non-rationality of it, while the unconverted is offended by the same situation?

In the former sort of position, common to Catholic and Protestant rationalism, grace may be seen, somewhat crudely, as something like an injection which clears blurred vision. In the latter, more often linked with voluntarist or fideist[1] accounts, it is not the vision, but the *will* which is moved by some kind of supernatural prompting. The actual mechanics of grace have been variously presented. Some restrict its sphere of operation firmly to the sacramental life of the Church. Some see it as working immediately and 'spiritually in the heart'. Others again locate it primarily in the efficacy of the scriptures in creating faith. What all these positions have in common is the implication that grace is something distinct and separate from nature, operating only in certain contexts, via certain media.

Doubtless for some people this account of faith is vindicated by the mere fact that some traditional authorities endorse it (though New Testament scholars and church historians might do a handy demolition job on allegations of any *single* traditional position). In chapter 4, however, it was argued that

[1] Positions suggesting that belief is a matter of a leap of 'sheer volition' or 'sheer faith' no rational proof being available or even desirable.

authorities are not justified simply by making the claim to be authorities. They have to offer some warrant for their claims. We must therefore examine what can be said for or against the traditional account.

Perhaps the strongest point in its favour is that it does some justice to the believer's conviction that his faith is a *response* to some initiating movement in God. To one actually believing, the ground of his assurance of and commitment to God seems to be that God presents himself as credible. Especially if he has any lively sense of 'the presence of God', it will be natural for him to extrapolate, and attribute the very generation of his belief to, divine activity. His perspective is something of a lover's insisting that all the love in him is called into being only by the other's existence.

In addition, it is often the case, as a matter of psychological fact, that religious belief 'clicks' all of a sudden. James's *Varieties of Religious Experience* documents scores of cases, some verging on religious pathology or parapsychology, where faith comes with irresistible immediacy. People grasp at metaphors to articulate the phenomenon: scales fall from their eyes; day breaks; pennies drop; things leap into focus. The overwhelmingness of the conviction and the apparent passivity of the believer before it make images of realities 'borne in from beyond' seem peculiarly apt.

The psychological compellingness of a conviction, however, is no guarantee of its supernatural origin. In terms of the experienced quality of the 'conversion' there seems no clear way of isolating religious belief, or at least not any given religious belief. Intense and dramatic and transforming experiences occur in many fields, religious and non-religious. Marghanita Laski documents some of them in her analysis of ecstasy, and as far as one can judge through the regularizing framework of the questionnaire she uses, 'the same experience' arises in many contexts which have little else in common. In response to nature, political options, human need, art, their own vocation in life, people are liable to overwhelming, disruptive and powerfully motivating experiences. There seems nothing in the sheer *feel* of it to isolate religious belief from all the others. Indeed it is hard to specify how one *could* recognize 'by the feel of it' any experience qualitatively different from *every* other. But if it

82

isn't possible to distinguish religious belief phenomenologically from any other, is it not simply by dogmatic interpretation that it can be held to be different?

Dogmatic interpretations, of course, may be right. There is not, however, any obvious way of isolating 'religious experience' as so qualitatively different from everything else that a supernatural source has to be postulated for it. Indeed it is arguable whether such isolable experiences are even *necessary* to 'the faith of a Christian believer'. Unless the term is limited to James's 'twice born', belief arises and sustains itself in many people who are never overwhelmed by any vivid sense of the presence of God, or aware of specific 'religious experiences'. If it is the 'immediate operation of the grace of God' which effects faith in such cases too, it cannot be by virtue of 'such-a-big-bang-it-must-be-God' conversions, but by some less conspicuous and less episodic energy.

Is it then just a superfluous hypothesis that the occurrence of belief requires grace? Is grace a kind of phantom force allegedly interrupting the natural psychic processes of the human, but empirically undetectable? Is there any good reason for holding that it is the effective cause of belief, when the combined insights of sociology, psychology, history and philosophy seem enough to explain why people believe what they do? Is it plausible to suggest that men come to all the other religious beliefs under the sun by 'natural processes' but in the case of one chosen faith arrive at it by grace? Does grace in any case exclude natural processes, or is it 'something' which can work *through* natural processes such as thinking, reflecting, judging, etc.?

The question of the origin of belief is closely linked to a central problem for any theology which affirms a God active in the world. In what sense is God 'behind' anything? If the best analogies are from the impersonal activity of physics or chemistry then it is hard to avoid pantheistic accounts of a God who is in, with and under everything. But then a pantheistic God in the end becomes redundant, just *because* he is everywhere.

If, on the other hand, the best analogies are from personal, discriminating presence—if God is here but not there, if he acts here but not there—other problems arise. Can such selective presence or activity be reconciled with other things which theologians are concerned to say about God? If the responsibility for faith or unfaith in men rests with God, and depends on his giving or withholding of effective self-disclosure, can any notion of his goodwill towards the world be coherently expounded? Not only is one tempted to say with the rhymster:

> How odd
> of God
> to choose
> the Jews.

One is tempted also to say 'How nasty!' How incredible that a God alleged to be and to will the supreme good of his creatures, and uniquely able to communicate that good to them, should allow the persistence of such doubt and disbelief and false belief to permeate the world if any one faith is true. The calamities of natural evil are not more distressing for the apologist setting out to justify the ways of God to men than the extent of unbelief.

For the non-believer, the distribution of belief and unbelief may be a curiosity, or even a matter of deep concern. In his passion for the truth he may wonder how on earth men can be duped by such nonsense as the traditional religious faiths affirm. He may find that psychological or sociological explanations hardly account for the situation, and be baffled by the persistent belief of apparently honest and rational men. His framework, however, does not permit the raising of the question, 'Why is belief allowed?' for there is, *ex hypothesi*, no one to allow it, or disallow it. He cannot go beyond the naturalistic question, 'How is belief explained?'

A traditional theistic framework, on the other hand, not only permits but demands the question, 'How is disbelief allowed?' and no theological account of faith can ignore the stress of the question. Belief and unbelief cannot be responsibly discussed in theological terms apart from the problem of evil.

Even within the co-ordinates of traditional discussions of course, the problem of unbelief has been variously 'solved'. (For the moment we will assume that from the 'orthodox' Christian standpoint there are analogous difficulties about atheism and agnosticism and about non-Christian religious beliefs, though that begs a large question. In traditional discussions, however, Hindus and sceptics have been equally easily classified as 'infidels', and by any strong 'orthodox' standard belief in anything which is not Christianity is 'unbelief'.)

One 'solution' is to deny that responsibility for unbelief is God's, and to lay it squarely at man's door. It is human freedom, on this view, which refuses belief; God is there to be seen and known, but man wilfully disbelieves, and grows hard in his resistance to the possibility of God. Intellectual self-deceit, deliberate refusal to face his incompleteness, various cultivated defences all insulate him from the currents of divine self-disclosure, and in the end he is firmly entrenched in an unbelief of his own making.

This sort of account raises all the difficulties voiced earlier about the idea of choosing belief. Is this alleged freedom a supernatural reality to be affirmed in the face of all the apparent concrete restrictions which a man encounters? Does he ever have pure responsibility for what he believes? Is the claim, anyway, that individuals are responsible for their own scepticisms and errors? Or is it rather that society is somehow collectively responsible for the creation of a world where belief is naturally implausible for so many individuals? In either case the 'freedom' realized by someone born and reared in a limited context and under the various pressures of human existence is so tenuous that it can hardly be identified with the radical cosmic independence attributed to those who deny God.

Divergent speculations about human responsibility for evil are explored in the Judaeo-Christian traditions through interpretations of the 'Fall' narrative. Whether unfallen bliss is seen as an actual historical condition of man once upon a time, or whether it is taken as an image of his potential, or a symbol of his future, these traditions grapple with the distance between man's present and his longed-for condition.

If man himself is *not* fully responsible for that distance but is as born into it as he seems to be, its occurrence is a major theological problem. Does someone else impose it on man? If God, then is his goodwill not as equivocal as any doctrine of predestination can make it? If not God, then is his 'responsibility' for the world not so equivocal that no doctrine of creation can be cashed out?

Some theologians resist all such questions as manifesting the

85

horrid pride of tidy-minded rationalists seeking to trim God to their mental size. Speculation on these mysteries is, they imply, at best pointless and at worst a repetition of Eve's lust for the forbidden fruit. Such wondering is provoked, however, not merely by existentially remote questions like 'What happened at the beginning of things?', but by claims intended as directly relevant to the *salvation* of the world. For *if* God has saved or is saving the world, and *if* knowledge of God is part at least of the meaning of salvation, the persistence of doubt or unbelief jeopardizes, as much as the persistence of death or fear, the confidence that we are saved. The apparent impossibility of Christian belief for so many people cannot be registered with cool equanimity by anyone who holds that belief is 'of grace', or is an intrinsic part, far less a condition, of salvation.

Of course some accounts of how grace 'overcomes' disbelief are theologically no improvement on the bad news of invincible unfaith. Hints of mind-bending or hidden persuasion are sinister, and if God's effect on human belief can be depicted only in terms of subliminal, quasi-hypnotic suggestion by the Holy Spirit, theology is in a parlous state. Not only would such alleged operations be empirically undetectable, they would reduce man to a thing acted upon, and so trivialize any doctrine of creation. There are major questions for any theology about the adequacy of using language of personal intervention as the primary analogy for the impinging of the transcendent on human life. But if it *is* the language of persons which best explores one's theological horizon, one would hope for less vulgarity of religious imagination than the overtones of hypnotism, blackmail or irresistible magnetism as modes of divine persuasion suggest. All God-talk may be inadequate. Personal God-talk may be inadequate in a distinctive way. But if it is personal God-talk that is settled for, whatever its limits, then it must be at least the *best* personal talk available. Images of grace, for instance, should be no less courteous than George Herbert's poem 'Love', or no less delicate than Kierkegaard's king with his beggar-maid.

The more basic worry though is about the whole concept of divine action within which 'grace' has its theological home. Can any talk of grace avoid the horns of a nasty dilemma? On the one hand, there is the suggestion of particular interferences by God in some but not all situations. It is taken, for example, as easier to explain how God changes minds than how he changes physical structures, but the problem is not eased by this suggestion, and, in view of the psychosomatic unity of people, even intensified. For if God interrupts at all the mental or physical processes of the world his operation seems irretrievably random (if impersonal) or arbitrary (if personal). If, on the other hand, God is thought to be equally involved everywhere in the world simultaneously, talk of his activity loses all focus. He is so constantly present in all situations that he has no special engagement in any.

The argument so far has suggested that when we give a little tug at the notion of faith, we unravel a whole skein of theological problems about God, grace, freedom, providence and salvation. This is within the context of Christian theology.

The position is further complicated by the fact that parallel claims to explain belief and unbelief occur in most religious traditions and appear to compete. Thus, precisely what the Christian claims to believe 'to his salvation' the Muslim takes as precise evidence of his lack of Allah's grace, or his defective understanding. The very commitment to vulnerability which is central in Christian tradition is a sign of *un*enlightenment to some forms of Buddhism. The Hindu faith that all truths, however apparently contradictory, are reconcilable in an ultimate truth scandalizes the Christian who finds in his faith the rejection of other religious traditions.

Thus the believer who claims that his belief is 'of grace' is not only faced with the need to reconcile the ongoing convictions of atheists and agnostics with his understanding of God, he is also soon stranded in some kind of commitment to the superiority of his faith *vis-à-vis* others. Not only is such imperialism distasteful to anyone with genuine awareness of the depth and range of another faith, it is almost ridiculous when one takes a bird's eye view of the growth and development of religious traditions. What was God 'doing' in eighth century B.C. China, while inspiring the prophets of Israel and the Jews who believed them? How can the faith of Israel be isolated from the cultural traditions which fed into it and seem palpably to have modified it in various ways? What are the theological implications of any claim that God gives himself here and not there?

The question can be focused even more narrowly. For within Christianity itself there is no monolithic content to the faith which has 'carried with it complete conviction'. Does God, then, in grace inspire different people to different beliefs, or are only some would-be Christians Christian? There have been many references and allusions in this book so far to various Christian beliefs, but is there an identifiable centre to Christian belief as such?

This is the issue which we must look at more closely in the following chapter, considering how the identity of belief is related to the tradition which mediates it.

Meanwhile, however, does anything survive of the claim that belief is 'of grace'? It seems so problematic an affirmation that it is hard to see even what is at stake between its acceptance and its denial. For man, the issue is how his freedom and his nature relate to his openness to God and God's impact on him. With reference to God, the issue is how, if he acts, his operation creates new situations without violating the autonomy he has supposedly conferred on the world in creating it. Both problems require far larger and subtler consideration than they can be given here, and less crude exploration of the traditional suggestion that true belief is a result of grace. All that can be said from the scope of this discussion is that the questions need to be raised; and if the notion of grace is either dismissed or accepted without scrutiny, the understanding of belief may be significantly the poorer.

DISCUSSION QUESTIONS

Do you think religious belief is significantly different from other beliefs in terms of how it comes to you? If so, what are the differences?

Do you think it is easier or harder to explain the varieties of religious belief if faith has a 'supernatural' origin?

FOR FURTHER READING

K. Barth, 'The Revelation of God as the Abolition of Religion' in O. S. Thomas, ed., *Attitudes Toward Other Religions*. S.C.M. Forum Books.

C. Davis, *Christ and the World Religions*. Hodder.

9

BELIEF AND TRADITION

Thus People's Liberal is a church designed to meet the
needs of today, and to serve the whole man. This includes
the worship of God free of outmoded theological definitions
and palatable to a mind come of age in the era of Relativity.
'It is the final proof of God's omnipotence that he need not
exist in order to save us', Mackerel had preached ...

PETER DE VRIES   *The Mackerel Plaza*

Most religions which are now established as 'world faiths' have a
long history. They have survived centuries of cultural change.
They have been transplanted into new situations. They have
been adopted by men worlds apart from their original apostles.
How in this kind of context does one decide whether one shares
the *same* faith as one's fathers?

Suppose one tries to reconstruct the faith of a Christian living in Antioch early in the second half of the first century A.D.
What is he likely to believe?

He is firmly convinced of a God who has chosen the Jews as
his special people from the beginning of history, and who has
significantly intervened in their history, guiding the patriarchs,
leading his people out of Egypt where they were slaves. In recent
days, within his father's memory, God has made his most
decisive intervention by sending Jesus as his Messiah. This man
was born of a virgin, and his birth was marked by remarkable
astronomical phenomena. He grew to manhood, escaping death
in infancy only by God's direct intervention. He began his active
ministry after God's spirit marked him out during his baptism
by John the Baptist. He then went around healing and teaching,
and doing amazing miracles which showed his power over
nature and vindicated his authority. His challenge to the established religious authorities led them to plot his death, and he
was crucified on trumped-up charges, having fulfilled many

prophecies made in the Jewish Scriptures about God's Messiah. His obedience in suffering even death in faithfulness to God's will caused his Father to vindicate him by raising him bodily from the dead, to eye-witnesses of our believer's grandfather's generation. Although many of that generation had died, it was expected that before all did, the Risen Jesus would come again to judge the world, and establish finally the kingdom of God which his life, ministry, death and resurrection had initiated.

Then suppose one reconstructs the possible belief of an Alexandrian Christian in the fifth century. For him, God is the threefold unity of Father, Son, Spirit in coeternal communion. Although not ceasing to participate in this Godhead which constitutes his identity, the second 'person' of the Trinity, sometimes called the Logos of God, had miraculously taken to himself the human nature of men, by the power of the Spirit being born of a woman, Mary, as the man Jesus, and living and dying in that human capacity. Since, however, his incarnation had bound the perishing human nature of men inseparably to the undying life of God, death could not finally destroy him, and he rose. In this, he anticipated the future of all the cosmos, which was, in virtue of his full belonging to it, able to be caught up into the life of God.

Next take the faith of a twelfth-century Italian accepting the teachings of his Church. For him, God has created the world, and man has abused his rational freedom by sinning against God in defiant pride. The punishment due to him is death, and God's inexorable holiness cannot turn a blind eye to the enormity of man's misdeeds. He is reluctant to allow man to perish, however, since that would be the undoing of his creation. He therefore persuades his son to become man and pay the penalty of man's sin, taking the guilt and punishment of humanity on his own shoulders. By this sacrifice, willingly undertaken, the demands of justice are satisfied while the power of divine love overcomes the evil will of Satan to destroy man, and redeems him for eternal bliss, covered by the merits of his crucified Saviour. Through the Sacraments of the Church, the means of grace instituted by Jesus, these merits are made available to the faithful, so that they can be confident that even the holy God will countenance their acceptance into heaven,

90

finding their sin cancelled by the greater obedience of his only son.

Finally, consider a twentieth-century radical Existentialist Christian. He believes that 'God' is the word by which, in the past, men have focused their ultimate concerns of life, death, guilt, hope. They must now learn to discard the word as a superfluous remnant of former cosmology. The man Jesus, using the cosmological framework of his day, liberated men from the crippling elements of their existence. He lived with such freedom and outgivingness towards all he encountered that not even his death could destroy his impact, and the community inspired by him still find themselves quickened to hope that such love as he communicated is stronger than death. The world is responsible for its own destiny. No divine miraculous interventions occur. To say 'Jesus is God' is not to affirm a supernatural event of incarnation. It is to accept that in the man Jesus, the ultimate concern of man is clarified and that the clue to the meaning of human existence is offered.

Each of these thumbnail sketches is, of course, incapable of representing an age. Individuals might reject or modify at least some of the theological 'norms' of their own day. Professional theologians might refine beyond recognition the bald credal outlines demanded of the rank-and-file. In any one period there would be disputes about interpretation, people modestly or cynically 'going along with' dogmas they found unintelligible and irrelevant, or firmly adhering to misunderstood 'bastard' versions of official teaching.

All that can be allowed, perhaps, for our four constructs is that, in a stylized way, they pick out some central features of their contemporary theological worlds which were being emphasized at those times.

But if that is so, if the doctrinal content of the faith in the first, fifth, twelfth and twentieth centuries was anything like that, how can we possibly talk of a *common* belief, of sharing the *same* faith? If, in addition, we consider the shifts in attitude and practice, there seems even less common ground. The Inquisition which could once be regarded as the organ of divine providence now seems to most Christians a monstrous institution. Today few Christian sensibilities could endorse crusades. Many would be squeamish even about Christian judgements that other religions are false which would have been axiomatic in most earlier times. Ethical standards have shifted. No Christian now would accept slavery as a legitimate social option, whereas many would welcome sexual freedoms deplored by earlier periods. Some Christian groups have been firmly pacifist, while some bishops have blessed battleships and prayed for the destruction of enemies. At times Christianity has manifested itself through communist practices with regard to property, while Protestant Christendom has been identified as a main pillar of capitalism.

This variety of doctrine and practice is unnerving. Whether or not believing is choosing, or acting, being struck 'from outside' by something, being conditioned to certain attitudes or having a disposition to respond in certain ways to certain questions, it must have a content. Christian belief (or, for that matter, Hindu or Muslim belief) can't be believing just *anything*.

But how does one draw lines? How does one say, 'Well, here Christian belief stops and something else starts?' Must a Christian believe absolutely everything which his tradition has affirmed? But that's impossible, for some of the beliefs contradict each other. Are there one or two central doctrines comprising 'the substance of the faith', and a lot of optional peripheral ones? Has the substance then been constant from the beginning? Does any single strand carry right through, or is the tradition more like a spun rope, where none of the strands runs the whole length? But then, in virtue of what is it the *same* rope?

The question is not just a philosophical one about the identity of things. People are often anxious about whether or not they belong to the Christian faith. Groups excommunicate groups, and wars rage around the question of who belongs inside or outside. The identity problem is not merely abstract or academic. It is a human issue.

When two contemporaries meet, they have the chance of interrogating each other. With patience and goodwill each one can begin to get the feel of the other's vocabulary and style of thought. One can learn that such and such a word has negative overtones for the other, or that he uses X precisely as the majority use Y. Understanding, if it is to emerge at all between people on the intellectual level, depends on such exchanges.

With the past, understanding is more difficult. Documents have a sort of frozenness about them. A good historian, with subtlety and imagination, can reconstruct a good deal, both of the background and of the specific context of any statement of belief. But the give and take is impossible.

Suppose, for instance, that one was trying to establish New Testament belief about the resurrection. Obviously we have the stories, some of them at least suggesting a bodily resurrection. Did they really believe that? Well, why else would they tell the stories? Only because they thought a television camera crew could have filmed the stone being moved, and the risen Christ emerging? Or because that was their only available *idiom* for saying that this Jesus who had died was for them alive still— alive as God was alive, *not* bodily, but somehow continuous and discontinuous with the Jesus they had known.

If we could cross-examine the editors of the gospels, and make them understand what we mean by historical accuracy (a concept which is almost certainly an anachronism for any pre-Renaissance historian) how would they answer our questions about the resurrection? Would they say 'Of course you couldn't have shown it on TV documentary if a camera crew had happened to be around', or would they insist 'Unless a Television News team could, in principle, have filmed the emergence from the tomb, our faith is vain'?

Because the past is inaccessible beyond a certain point, answers have to be tentative and speculative. They may, however, make quite a difference to how one relates one's own belief to the tradition. If I think that the first Christians really found the literal emptiness of the tomb central to their faith, then I can hardly say with integrity that I share their faith, at least on that point. If, on the other hand, I can be convinced that the synoptic narratives of the empty tomb are religious legends, told to present an image of the living presence of Christ *in spite of* the fact that the body lay in the tomb, then I have more confidence that I may share their faith.

The theological 'continuity' would then depend on my ability to articulate their central 'faith/experience' and to establish analogies between it and my own. It may be hard to believe the tomb was empty. It is almost harder to suggest how any identification of 'the risen Christ' is possible without reference

93

to the identity of the body which was the body of Jesus. Can a person be himself without his body? Is the body of the risen Christ identical with the body of Jesus? Certainly when a believer says he is aware of Christ in his life now as a present reality, he is not talking about the body of Jesus. But then how does he identify the one he 'knows' as Christ? What is it he actually experiences? Is it a voice or a vision which announces itself as Jesus the Christ? Or is it a less specific sense of freedom or support or challenge or hope which seems to come from deeper resources than the community knows itself to have at its disposal? And is this discovery of new human possibilities then interpreted *as* the presence of Christ, because these seem analogous to the possibilities Jesus presented in his time to his contemporaries?

Again answers must be speculative. There is no way of cross-questioning Paul, say, on what his experience of the risen Christ was really like. People do experience release from guilt. They learn to live with themselves and others, and sometimes in Christian contexts. They find, in Tillich's famous phrase, 'the courage to be'. The question is whether these are precisely the experiences which provoked early Christians to speak in terms of living in Christ and having him live in them.

Of course rationalization is easy here. I may just be reluctant to concede that people *could* believe such impossible things in the past of the tradition I belong to. Or I may hate to face the possibility that I am excluded from experiences which others had and have. Or I may simply be frightened at the implications of what different worlds the past and the present are. For all these reasons, I may tend to underestimate the discontinuity between the past of my tradition and my own belief. I may claim analogies too glibly, and make facile assumptions that when they said one thing they *really meant* another.

If, on the other hand, I too easily assume that the past of the tradition is totally unlike the present, because its *accounts* of itself are quite different, I may be mistaking the surface for the substance. There may be real points of contact where the human issues with which past theological tradition wrestled are perennial ones confronting our generation also. It may be that their use of myth or legend, or even of popular superstition, has a *raison d'être* worth pursuing. Simply to dismiss the material

94

for not being scientifically or historically plausible may be premature.

There are major divisions within the contemporary Christian community as to whether such interpretation of the faith 'behind' the statements is possible, or necessary. Indeed, even that assertion is prejudging, for some members of the Christian Church consider that those on the other side of the divide from them are actually ruled out as members. At one extreme is the perspective of those who insist that not a jot or tittle of the original faith must be abandoned by anyone legitimately entitled 'Christian'. For them it is a firmly restricted and exclusive term, and any modification or reinterpretation of any article of faith is a deviation from the normative position. At the other extreme are those who suggest that one can be a true successor of the original faith while rejecting most of even .its central doctrines, the existence of God, for instance, or the divinity of Christ, or the possibility of life after death. In between there is a whole spectrum of positions, more or less insistent on a minimal required content of faith, with varying degrees of flexibility on what is dispensable.

The main difficulty about the first position is that contemporary biblical scholarship makes it increasingly hard to identify a single 'original faith'. It looks instead as if we have in the New Testament several traditions interpreting the life and significance of Jesus in a variety of ways. As far back as the first century, some of these interpretations seem to be coherent alternative accounts, rather than being parts of one whole picture which can be assumed as a unity. It is *possible* to conflate all the New Testament documents by more or less sophisticated exegesis. The result, however, wins its alleged unity at the price of many chinks and forced connections. It is rather like trying to jam six rather different jigsaw puzzles of one scene into a single unified picture.

Most of the New Testament writers or editors were not, of course, selfconscious about 'the unity of the Scriptures'. The New Testament did not exist as even a formal collection until much later than most of its components. Each writer was concerned to give his own account of the tradition as it came to him or as he experienced it, but was far less able than our own generation of historians to take a synoptic view of the

95

different strands of the emergent faith. By the time one comes to the biblical interpretation of the high Patristic period of the fourth and fifth centuries, and from then on until fairly recent times, it can be taken for granted that Scripture is a unified canon, incapable of contradicting itself. Only the rise of critical history makes it possible convincingly to defend another position.

Furthermore, many of the New Testament traditions are philosophically fairly unselfconscious. Myth, imagery and parable are characteristic modes of expression, and their implications cannot always be translated into corresponding prose. If poetry could be paraphrased adequately, there would be little point in writing it, and at least parts of the New Testament are plausible candidates for such irreducibility. The visions of the eschatological Kingdom of God are not, for example, astrological predictions worth calculating cataclysms from. When a story recounts the ascension of Christ this need not constrain us to imagine extraordinary powers of vertical take-off. On this point, several past exegetes have been much more sensitive than heavy-footed rationalists, who attack or defend the scriptures as if they were the front page of *The Times* or even Plato's *Republic*. If a document is written in one genre it is liable to be distorted if read as another, no matter how scrupulous the attention to its internal detail. And within the New Testament many types of material occur, and deserve a variety of approaches.

So far, only historical or literary objections have been made to the position commonly called 'fundamentalist'. These might be supplemented by theological ones. Would it not suggest some sort of paralysis in an allegedly lively God if he were to communicate himself only through first-century terms or concepts? Could history really have the value implied in a doctrine of creation if all its significance was confined to the little space from about 4 B.C. to A.D. 29? Might one not query so literalistic an interpretation of Scripture as the key to a life highly ambivalent in its relation to the law? If Jesus was free to upset the scribes and Pharisees, is he not likely to be misrepresented by any suggestion that he is bound by the book? How could one consistently celebrate Paul's rejection of physical circumcision while insisting on an attitude to the Bible that came little short of intellectual castration?

It is easy, however, to take knocks at conservative biblicism. The more demanding task is to find a coherent intellectual alternative account of the identity of Christian faith. Not all fundamentalists, of course, are fundamentalist about Scripture. One may find Thomist fundamentalists, who give to St Thomas Aquinas the status some allow only to Scripture; or Nicene or Chalcedonian fundamentalists who insist on those particular formulations of historic Creeds as absolutely normative. In the latter cases, of course, there is even less historical plausibility about the suggestion that these theologies represent 'the original faith'. This is not, however, a fatal objection, unless one shares the biblicist conviction that nothing in Scripture *can* be improved upon theologically.

We cannot here embark on a critique of the various historic creeds of the Church. Suffice it to suggest that any confidence about continuity in doctrine has shaky foundations. The fact that people have said the same words for centuries is no guarantee that they believe the same things. Under cover of the words various interpretations and reinterpretations go their different ways. Few people now saying the creeds believe them in the same way as the Fathers who formulated them. The gap is not often a matter of deliberate hypocrisy, though one can do nice parodies of mental rewriting going on as people chant uneasily in unison. More often, people just do not know what either the Fathers or they themselves mean by the words they say. It is the act of speaking it together which maintains their identity, not the fact that they all understand it in a common way.

Even if one disputes, however, about the actual doctrinal unity of the church, fundamentalists of any sort have a clear reference point by which to identify at least themselves, even if they tend to submit all would-be fellow Christians to a doctrinal Procrustean bed. Can 'Liberals' or 'radicals' do likewise, or are they only identified parasitically as being non-fundamentalists? (To bracket liberal and radical together is in many ways impossible. Each carries *odium theologicum* and *politicum* for the other, and there are important differences. They are, though, it seems to me, alike in their search for a theological 'hard centre'.)

The two most likely candidates for the theological centre might seem to be God and Jesus. Attractively, in some ways, the suggestion is made that no human propositions at all should be given such central status as the creeds have had. The unity of the faith is in God, and particularly in the love of God articulated in Jesus.

But who is God? Liberals and radicals are liable to part at this point, since many radicals find the concept of God no longer meaningful or theologically useful. Theologies of the secular, new essences of Christianity, death of God movements, all find classical theism dispensable. What is more, some at least of those who embrace such atheism are sure that it is the truest successor in the twentieth century of the genuine Christian tradition. Belief in a God, they suggest, is as much a cultural hangover and a religious bondage as was the Pharisaic obsession with the law. The only focus for Christianity is Christ. (But does 'Christ' make sense without 'God'?)

Many on the other hand find 'God' a word which still belongs without strain in their vocabulary. Their difficulty, perhaps, is to articulate any distinctively *Christian* concept of God. Monotheism is clearly shared at least by Jews and Muslims, and a liberal Christian theism can be far more accommodating towards at least these other faiths than can strict Trinitarian theology.

But who *is* the God of Christianity? Is he 'whatever Jesus believed in'? Is he 'that than which nothing greater can be conceived'? Is he the 'First Cause' of the universe? Is he the presupposition of my being human? Is he a Jesus-shaped blow-up, conceivable only as a vast cosmic person? Is he pure spirit? Can he be all these things simultaneously?

Obviously, *if* monotheism is true, there is only one God to be believed in and whatever men say of him or think of him, or however variously they pray to him, he is the transcendent reality to which they relate. *A fortiori* then, if *Christians* now think or speak differently of him from *Christians* then, he is still the same God. This understanding affords a good base for ecumenism, contemporary and retrospective. (Though it may sometimes be a more sinisterly disguised piece of imperialism: 'You know, you chaps, it's really our god you're believing in all the time'.) It even allows one to move into the field of interfaith contact, with the same caveat about theological take-overs.

But even if God is the same, men believe differently in him, and believe different things about him. The Christian community, though it may piously affirm that its true identity, like anyone else's, lies with God, actually tries to find itself empirically by defining true Christian belief. And on this level, everyone cannot be right. God cannot both be Trinitarian and non-Trinitarian. Though he may accept even those who have got him wrong, whichever he is.

Debate about God still rages, and while it does, it is extremely difficult to work out criteria for 'the same faith'. Nor are things much easier when it comes to Jesus. Men believe differently about what is historically knowable. Further, they disagree about how *important* it is to have historical knowledge or strong probability. For some, the admiration of a human life consistently lived as that one was is sufficient basis for the religious esteem in which Jesus must be held, and for his claim on present practical allegiance. For others, Jesus is only of interest if not merely man but also God, and the 'humanism' of many liberal statements is anathema.

Thus the questions about *which* faith is true persist, even if theologically they are not to be regarded as the question on which one's destiny hangs. *Can* Jesus be both the son of Mary and Joseph and the second person of the Trinity incarnate? If not, which is he? If so, how is he? Can Scripture be right about a second coming, or is that a piece of apocalyptic mythology? Will people live after they die, or must they learn to find the whole meaning of their existence in the time and space between now and their deaths? Can they worship in this way, or is their worship invalid unless conducted by such-and-such priests in the official mode? Should men evangelize in the conviction that men are damned unless they know and affirm the truth, or is that primitive and obsolete theology? Is the notion that men are damned for *anything* consistent with the Christian understanding of God or not?

Discussion of 'the nature of belief' thus forces one to consider one's perspective on the tradition and one's relation to it. The term 'Christian belief' may be used more or less restrictively, and debate *about* the usage is part of the disagreement *in* belief which occurs within the Churches. How one comes to terms with the issue of belief and tradition will depend on one's total stance theologically, and cannot be discussed apart from that. But the rest of one's theological stance will at least imply some relation to the question of tradition, and awareness of what that is may help to clarify one's overall position.

From some strongly committed theological positions, there can be only one theology, and the rest are non-starters. From other strongly committed theological positions there is a fair range of doctrinal options, all within the umbrella of 'Christian faith'. For the observer of religious traditions, who has no theological axe to grind, the 'Christian faith' is probably an umbrella term for all those institutions, practices and dogmas which call themselves 'Christian'. The diversity of the traditions can then be acknowledged without completely blurring the distinction between Christian belief and non-Christian belief. One may have a strong theological conscience about accepting such a permissive and all-embracing identification of 'Christian belief'. In that case one is bound to see many of the self-designated Christians as false pretenders to the title, and to rule them out by applying a more stringent and restrictive account of Christianity. If that is not the case, however, the broader identification seems to offer a better starting-point for discussion than more rigid definition, which puts a theological stranglehold on many positions that have aimed at being 'Christian belief' and thought of themselves as such.

DISCUSSION QUESTIONS

What things would you say a man *had* to believe if he was to be properly called a Christian?

Do you think there is an absolute authoritative way of settling questions of Christian doctrine? If so, what is it? If not, how would you decide that you belonged to the same tradition as anyone in the Christian past?

FOR FURTHER READING

Bertrand Russell, *Why I am not a Christian*, Chapter 1. Allen & Unwin.
John Knox, *The Limits of Unbelief*. Collins.
John Bowden, *Who is a Christian?*. S.C.M. Press.

10

THE POSSIBILITY OF BELIEF

'I mean,' persisted the housekeeper, 'didn't anybody bother
with your religious education?'

Miss Hare was too embarrassed to answer.

'So as you can believe. You do believe in *something*, don't
you?'

Miss Hare hesitated. Then she said, very slowly:

'I believe. I cannot tell you what I believe in, any more
than what I am. It is too much. I have no proper gift. Of words,
I mean. Oh yes, I believe! I believe in what I see and what I
cannot see. I believe in a thunderstorm, and wet grass, and
patches of light, and stillness. There is such a variety of good.
On earth. And everywhere.'

'But what is over it?' Mrs Jolley had to burst out.

'That!' Miss Hare cried. 'That! I would rather you did not
ask me about such things.'

PATRICK WHITE *Riders in the Chariot*

Last chapters are notorious in the field of apologetics. Would-be
defenders of the faith, having acknowledged the existence of
fiery philosophical, psychological and sociological dragons,
somehow do a theological outflanking movement, and seem to
slay them quietly from behind.

In addition, the tone frequently shifts from the coolly academic to the warmly or wistfully religious, and the author, having
set the scene as a mere purveyor of intellectual options, suddenly comes on stage as a live person. This puts unfair pressure
on the average gentlemanly British reader, who has decent hesi-
tations about marching with critical boots over anything as naked
as a fellow-creature's soul.

The indulgence of a personal statement is not, in this case,
likely to embarrass the reader, since it invites him to overhear,
not a blushing credo, but a running battle. In this fight, a
sceptical *alter ego* probably anticipates all the nastier criticisms

101

which the reader might be tempted to raise. The only natural form, therefore, in which this book can conclude itself is in schizophrenic disputation. Such an ending is humanly distressing, theologically unsatisfactory, and aesthetically distasteful. In its favour, all that can be said is that it is fairly honest, and may reflect some of the complexities which any more integrated view must encompass.

SNARL That's a typical evasion on your part, if I may say so. You can't admit you don't believe in case you upset the theologians. And you can't pretend you do, because you know that would be philosophically incoherent. So you retreat. Coward!

SWITHER You could be right. Certainly I'd like to be clearer one way or another. Straightforward atheism would simplify one's existence so much. It fits so many of the facts. It leaves nice uncluttered options like suicide, hedonism or liberal humanism. It's the practical stance of so many good people. Even straightforward faith would simplify it, and presumably make one happier. One wouldn't ever doubt if one's effort was worthwhile, or despair of good being stronger than evil. But I just *can't* opt for one or the other. I'm pulled both ways.

SNARL Yes, but for different reasons. All your intellect is on the side of atheism. But your contexts are Christian, and your emotional roots. To pull them up, as you rationally should, would be such a major upheaval that you prefer to stay where you are. But that's not belief. That's sheer evasion. You know you don't belong among the faithful.

SWITHER You mean because what I'm not sure about believing isn't in any case Christian belief?

SNARL Yes, exactly. You see, you have a guilty conscience. Even the things you'd like to be able to believe aren't what Christians accept. They believe in a personal God who made heaven and earth, who sent his son Jesus to live and die to save the world, and raised him from the dead. They believe Jesus now lives with God, who has sent his Spirit to be active in the world and to reveal the truth of God's salvation through the church. By their response to that revelation men will be judged, and those who believe will have eternal life, while the

102

rest are shut off from the presence of God. Now that's Christianity, take it or leave it. But don't be confused by these sly moderns who try to 'reinterpret' and finish up with a different creed altogether. Whether *they* interest you is another question. But you don't believe a word of orthodox Christianity.

SWITHER I can't say I believe it or not till you tell me more about what these words mean. The assertions are in such theological shorthand. You make it sound as if it were obvious what Christian belief was. But it isn't at all. And I doubt if it ever has been. I don't believe these affirmations are interpreted properly as accounts of fantastic cosmic events. They were made because people found their lives and deaths clarified. And I don't believe that's ever happened in relation to questions like whether silver teapots are circling the moon. So people who treat religious affirmations like that sort of assertion, and then rightly dismiss them, *must* be failing to understand what real religious convictions are.

SNARL You're just culturally blinkered. Of course people have *thought* fantastic cosmic entities affected their lives and deaths—demons and angels and witches and fairies. But we have no scruples about denying them. Why not let God go the same way?

SWITHER But you miss the point. You haven't understood the past if you just say, 'They believed in fairies and we don't'. Why should people start talking that way? What aspects of their existence constrained them to talk like that? Do we have better ways, for example, of linking beauty and power, or malice and ugliness, or of coming to terms with the apparent capriciousness of life? Believing that german measles in the pregnant mother causes blindness in unborn children obviously competes with believing that only syphilis in the father does. It is less clear that believing a demon causes it competes with either, though it may compete with believing God causes it.

SNARL As far as I'm concerned, the latter's an option between two positions which are either unintelligible or false. If people ever thought or think it a real choice, they are so different from me that we might as well belong to a different species. I'm not interested in communicating with them. They belong, as it were, to another world.

103

SWITHER I don't believe the worlds of human beings are so mutually impenetrable. I think it's usually worth taking seriously what other people find serious. Your position seems to me like finding the Rosetta stone and saying with alphabetic insularity, 'Meaningless scribbles!' These ways of talking were related to how people experienced life, no matter how inaccessible you now find them. When Christians say 'I believe in God', I don't believe they mean the world has an extra person in it, only big and transparent and invisible to many! That's not only implausible, it won't make sense of the way a believer organizes his life.

SNARL You're thinking of your university friends again. But ordinary believers now, like ordinary believers then, do believe precisely what you so rightly perceive to be implausible.

SWITHER Well, I doubt it. But if they do, then they aren't doing what I mean by believing in God.

SNARL Oh indeed! But you don't believe in him either.

SWITHER No! But if I come to, it won't be by bumping into a being I haven't happened to bump into yet. I'm sure of that.

SNARL You seem unusually decisive on that point. But if God isn't another being, how can he possibly be real?

SWITHER Well, for example, freedom's not a being, but it's real.

SNARL It's an abstraction. Is God an abstraction?

SWITHER Freedom's not an abstraction, except in certain situations. You ask a man in prison, or unhappily married, or obsessed with guilt, what freedom is. It's so real and concrete that he defines his existence in relation to it. Of course the word 'freedom' is, grammatically speaking, an abstract noun, but freedom is a reality which changes lives.

SNARL You're warming up to the sermon level of rhetoric. How does God change lives?

SWITHER I don't know if it makes sense to say he does, because I don't think that he can be isolated as a causal element in situations. But if we allow that idiom as a not inept metaphor,

104

he changes them in the direction of more hope, more truthfulness, less panic. He makes for life not measured out in coffee spoons. People can stop fighting to justify their own existences. They can risk loving and being loved.

SNARL Oh, more pieties! For goodness sake! Aren't you just saying 'Wherever I find the sort of thing I like in people, I call that "the effect of God" '? But that's a purely private definition. Just look at the people who actually claim with any confidence to be influenced by God. How many tight, smug, shrivelled people have you met, going around sure God has acted in their lives? If he has, you misjudge his effects. If he hasn't, isn't it more likely that all talk of God's effect is a kind of fantasy fulfilment, making up for the defects of their human existence? It's compensatory ego building, that kind of claim. Just as lonely children invent imaginary playmates, and sexual inadequates have fantasy lovers, 'God' is the fabrication of the humanly deficient.

SWITHER But that just doesn't fit the evidence. You can't say all religious believers are humanly deficient.

SNARL No, but a good lot are. And the ones who are not certainly don't represent more than the average number of decent, whole human beings in any group or any creed. Indeed, I think you might be able to make a case for saying religion breeds more fear and cant in people than it destroys.

SWITHER Only bad religion. But we were talking about *God's* effect on people, not religion's.

SNARL Oh, come on! Who is to do the distinguishing? The man who goes round in terror because he is sure God will thump him if he steps out of line is more sure he knows God than you are. What's more, the accredited sources of revelation agree with him. Who are you to say, from a basis of hypothetical speculation, that God *can't* be this or that?

SWITHER Well, men use the word to identify some reality which deserves wonder, adoration. You can't worship what is evil.

SNARL And who are you to say what's evil? It's precisely people

105

who have been convinced of the goodness of God who have gone round trembling.

SWITHER   Then they've misunderstood. God's goodness doesn't destroy or annihilate people. It creates them.

SNARL   Who says? That's liberal wishful thinking. The traditions in which God is alleged to disclose himself are quite insistent on the judgement of sinners who refuse to believe. How can you possibly claim to know God better than they did? You're at it again, merely projecting your moral prejudices on to the cosmos.

SWITHER   Now *you're* being ridiculous. The insight of prophets like Hosea, the instinct of millions of Christians, and the whole life of Jesus as we have it recorded are scarcely consonant with a picture of a God who thumps sinners.

SNARL   Not if you blame the redactors for all the nasty bits. But I'd have thought mainline tradition was that sinners only avoid thumping because Jesus takes the beating instead. There's no question of the penalty being waived. It's merely transferred. And Jesus and Paul and John all seem to assume a final judgement which discriminates among men.

SWITHER   No, it's inconceivable that God should sink to punishment.

SNARL   For one who doesn't pretend to know whether or not the deity exists, you're remarkably familiar with his ways. And in any case, haven't you lapsed into talk implying *a* being who does things?

SWITHER   Well, yes, but that's shorthand too, because human interaction seems in some ways to offer the best image of what I'm trying to articulate, that if God is, then he is for our good. But the trouble is, there would be a built-in inadequacy about articulating the transcendent. It would be hard to tell the difference between language which breaks down because it's struggling to express the inexpressible, and language which breaks down because it's common-or-garden nonsense. But there might be a difference.

SNARL   Look, how can you go on making these judgements?

One moment you admit you don't know if you're talking about anything. The next you're laying about you, demolishing other theological positions from a standpoint quite contrary to official Christian teaching. Then you adopt a traditional religious platitude about the ineffability of God to swipe philosophical critics with. What sort of private revelations do you claim?

SWITHER None. I'm just sure that God, if real, cannot be worse than the best I can imagine. And I know my better imaginings from my worse ones. They delight me.

SNARL My God, what conceit! So far you haven't said anything even coherent, far less better or worse. Discussing what God would be like if he existed seems to me a frivolous exercise. It disguises the hard fact that you have *no* conviction that he does exist. You've never encountered him, or anything remotely like a transcendental person. You find the world ambiguously good and evil, and know some situations where good seems quite impotent. Now, in my terms, that's *dis*belief. So why not just admit it without a ridiculous fuss, pack up this religious business and get on with living? That's a full-time job, which you're currently doing part-time because so much time and energy goes on this pointless speculation. Suppose there isn't God. Then you've just *got* to get on with it. Suppose there is. Well, if there is, he is, by definition, here now. And what difference is that making? You still have to get on with it, just the same.

SWITHER No, not just the same. If I really believed in God, it would make a huge difference.

SNARL What difference?

SWITHER Well, not a direct physical one, of course. Not even a psychological one, though it might do that too. But it would mean I would be entitled to hope my imagination wasn't exhausting the possibilities for the world's future.

SNARL That doesn't sound like much of a gain to me!

SWITHER You know that Dylan Thomas poem?

SNARL I find it suspicious that you can't say things in sober

107

prose. It's like preachers getting at the congregation via Browning!

SWITHER Damn it, I know it's suspicious! But it might also just be true that some things can be said only in poetry. Anyway, this one goes through a strange, haunting series of paradoxes:

Dead men naked they shall be one
With the man in the wind and the west moon.
Though they go mad they shall be sane,
Though they sink through the sea they shall rise again,
Though lovers be lost, love shall not,
And death shall have no dominion.

Now there is a difference between reading that poem as an expression of longing and reading it as a statement of truth. God is what makes that difference. Or, more accurately, 'God' is the word I use to name whatever it is or would be that could justify that difference.

SNARL But nothing justifies it. The poem is nonsense. Dead men naked are dead men naked. And if lovers are lost, love goes with them. The rest is mumbo-jumbo.

SWITHER Maybe. And yet I wonder. Some people seem so sure it's true, even though it strikes me as so impossible. How *can* they be so sure?

SNARL Oh, come on! There is no incompatibility, not even much rarity, about people being simultaneously convinced and deluded. We've been through all the Freudian evidence. You *know* it's possible.

SWITHER Yes, but it isn't just that. I mean just because belief is so suspect and extraordinary a possibility, given the way the world is, I feel the fact that it actually occurs deserves more attention. Of course some of it can be explained in terms of abnormal psychology. But some men of such awareness and insight in human terms also find it possible. They know the critical explanations. They know the depths of human chaos. But they still believe steadily. Now how can that be, unless they have some actual relation to a reality which convinces

108

them that it is more significant than all the misery of the world, and capable of transforming it?

SNARL Perhaps they have, but the reality might just be the concrete positive human love they've met in their early experience, which has made them steady people and gone into their bones. It's very hard to make a neurotic man out of a happy child. And if belief has been part of that basic, confident world, then it may well go on unchallenged. But it proves nothing theologically. In any case, if this 'reality' was something universal, why wouldn't we all be aware of it? Isn't it easier to believe no God exists, and that some men are lucky enough to find basic human security, than to believe God does exist and lets men live in anxiety for ignorance of him?

SWITHER Yes, I think it *is* easier to believe the former. But what interests me is that some people find themselves able to believe the harder thing, indeed, apparently, compelled to. What's more, some of them *do* display human qualities which seem to ring true to the image of new manhood suggested in Christian tradition. They *are* more alive. They *do* have freedom in face of the world and its more annihilating forces of hate, fear, isolation, guilt. Somehow they can see it with integrity, and yet not be deranged. They can live the next stage, whatever it brings, without frenzy.

SNARL But maybe they could do with a bit of frenzy. Anyone who has seen the death of a man at the hands of a man, let alone the monstrosities of our history, *should* be deranged. Those who know their present existence is directly or indirectly at someone else's expense damn well *should* be guilty. All this talk of atonement and 'acceptance as you are' is moral anaesthesia. Worrying about religious belief is not just an intellectual impossibility. It's a moral evasion.

SWITHER No, no, no! If it's that, it's not what I'm talking about. I'm talking about an awareness of things so delicate and acute and caring that it makes moral concern seem clumsy and distant. A condition of being human which makes me suspect that *not* worrying at it is the evasion. I feel almost like those detectives who feel uneasy when the solution seems obvious. There's a certain kind of simplicity which seems like oversimplification.

Of course I sometimes wonder if the whole thing is nonsense which can just be dropped without loss. Of course I can see all your arguments. And yet I find myself asking the question 'May you not, if you give up this issue, be like a man who decides, on the basis of some bad experience, that there is no such thing as real love?' From then on, he resists any serious use of the word, and keeps clear of any situation where he's liable to be disturbed by the possibility of being wrong. He cuts the world to the size he can cope with, intellectually and emotionally, and lives in it happily ever after. My suspicion is that any final drawing of a double line under the question of belief may be like that. One just comes to terms with the apparent limits of one's environment. And as a result one stops being open to all kinds of dimensions. In time they can no longer be seen, and so no longer explored.

SNARL But you don't even know what they might be, or how they are to be explored, or how you'd know you had found anything *en route*. So incoherent a possibility surely can't motivate you? I mean, I can see a man throwing himself out to test a daring hypothesis; but what *is* your hypothesis? That nonsense will become sense? That the impossible will become possible? It's not even coherent. And even if it were, entertaining a hypothesis is not believing.

SWITHER That depends on how you do it, surely. I'm certainly not talking about casual speculation, the way one entertains the possibility that there are little green men on Mars, or unknown rich uncles in Australia who may in the remote future die, and leave you unexpected fortunes. I mean investing yourself in the truth of the thing, being so involved in whether or not it's true that it changes who you are.

SNARL Oh, here we go again! As I see it, it changes you only for the worse. You waste so much good time on unanswerable questions, doing nothing for anyone, least of all yourself.

SWITHER No, I don't mean that sort of difference. It would be a total difference. I mean, if God is, I actually am *quite* different from who I am if he isn't.

110

SNARL What on earth does that mean?

SWITHER Well, if God is, I must be in relation to him, since that is part of what it means that he is God. Now there are big problems about why I'm unaware of that fact, if it is a fact. Can I be so blind or so stupid, or so trapped in my intellectual and emotional framework that I'm incapable of seeing what's there? I remember once reading about some remote tropical islanders who couldn't see a great battleship anchored off their island because they were only used to looking at boats twelve feet long? Can disbelief be like that? If it's not that, why shouldn't God be clear? And even if it is that, why, if God is good, does he not untrap me? Because he's deliberately with-holding himself? But that's impossible! He surely couldn't both know and will our good and leave us to a life of such destructive fretting. Or because his hiddenness could be for our good? Is that possible? Could we need his absence to grow, like adolescent fledglings nudged out of a parental nest? But that's impossible—that independence of God through forced ignorance of him could be better for us than ongoing knowledge of him. Surely that would be the *dis*integration of the Fall, the fate which D. H. Lawrence prayed against: 'Let me never know myself apart from the living God'.

SNARL You're getting hysterical! You're supposed to be telling me how you'd be quite different.

SWITHER I've just told you. If there is no God, then what I am is liable to disintegration. If God is, integrity is conferred on me again and again by his relating to me; and I can hope that the whole world has a future not determined by its present and its past.

SNARL But if God's busy conferring integrity on things at the moment, and they're in the state of *dis*integration they are currently in, it's not much of a benefit, is it?

SWITHER No. it can't be complete yet. I don't understand it, and I don't want to do a 'pie in the sky' future. But it's as if we were living on the obverse side of a possibility. You know what I mean? It's as if the non-presence of God, the dis-order of the world, were too palpable to be merely a natural fact. It's like the feel of a room which someone has left or will enter; one registers the non-presence as absence, not as non-existence.

SNARL That's just conditioning. You are acclimatized to mental images of God's presence—so you dramatize the discovery of his non-existence in terms of his 'disappearance'. You encounter no one. But you imagine yourself as a little twentieth-century Jacob, wrestling with an incognito God until he discloses himself. Well, go on if it's psychologically more exciting. But it's really shadow boxing. 'The absent God' is a myth dramatizing the unbelieving you. But every infant theologian knows that God is present everywhere all the time. He can't be absent. If he's not where you are, he's not God.

SWITHER But don't you think absence can be a mode of someone's presence with you?

SNARL Why will you play these word games? People are either there or not there, and why should God be different? Anyway, that's got nothing to do with whether or not you believe. You don't. You can't make up your mind whether God's absent or non-existent. I think you don't really expect to find him. You don't really believe he's going to become present at some future date. So stop pretending you're a believer in any sense. Entertaining the hypothesis that something may just possibly be the case is *not* believing.

SWITHER No, well I'm not sure that I'm saying I believe. I certainly don't, somehow, expect specific new experiences, like walking round the next corner, and bumping into someone who says, 'I'm God, you haven't met me before'. But I sometimes hope that I may see all that has happened to me in a different focus. And in some moods I really expect it.

SNARL Explain yourself. What 'different focus'?

SWITHER Well, take the parable of judgement in Matthew where the sheep and the goats are separated. In their lives, neither lot have had the slightest awareness of encountering Christ, or of responding negatively or positively. But when they see the situation with maximum awareness of its implications, it emerges that they actually have been encountering him and responding to him all along. Their whole human experience is

112

suddenly visible in a new light, namely as an ongoing relation to him. It's like finding what you've taken as a picture is really a three dimensional scene.

SNARL Another pious cliché!

SWITHER Well, occasionally, I feel as if I have possibilities of seeing my existence as far deeper than it appears to be. Instead of just saying, 'I am born, I will die. How will I live in between?', I find it possible to hope that I actually am involved responsively with God, even trusting 'him', though not as a distinct individual I can isolate, and not in ways I can yet specify.

SNARL But this is just the latest trendy form of Christian disbelief: God is other people. Or God is everything that happens. Are you so intellectually degenerate that you don't see that's pantheism? And a pantheist God is, in the end, so inert as to be redundant.

SWITHER I'm not saying that. You should listen before jumping to conclusions. If God isn't at some points significantly distinct from both people and nature, adoring him would be unthinkable. What I'm saying is that human community may be the only context in which I encounter God, not that God is exhausted by the limits of human community. But it would mean in practice that I shouldn't expect to find 'him' anywhere else. But then, even in the human world, he couldn't be indiscriminately identified with all that goes on. So much in the world works *against* human community: sickness and death; the instincts of men to stay apart from each other and be safe; the irreversibility of the past; the various uglinesses that make people naturally unloved. God is not in these things. His presence in the world is 'critical'. It is in the direction of overcoming death, of giving men freedom and safety enough to know each other and be known, of undoing the past, of conferring beauty on the unloved. So there is a difference made by God's reality, if he's real.

SNARL You're raving! These things are impossible, either contradictions in terms or sheer practical impossibilities. How can the past be undone, or death overcome? And when will men ever trust each other? You are having fantasies because you hate

113

to face the world as it sadly is. You believe, in your more lucid moments, that people die and rot; and you believe that they cannot be themselves except as bodies, which is to say they cannot 'be themselves' disembodied. You know they die separately, and trapped in the past, and ugly. You can't imagine the shape or structure of a heaven where all that could be undone.

SWITHER No, of course I can't. But I'm not even interested in a faith which claims less. I don't care about God as the first stage in an explanatory hypothesis of the world's existence. For that one might as well have an elephant on the back of a turtle. I don't even need him as a guarantor or enabler of moral decencies. These things stand on their own feet as human possibilities. I don't find it convinces me to be told that everything that happens is somehow part of the life of God. But what excited the Christians into extravagances of language about 'resurrection' or 'sanctification' or 'new creation' or 'justification' *except* such possibilities as I'm talking about? Only they seem to have been sure.

SNARL But you're not at all sure.

SWITHER No. I'm not. There seems such irony in it. They say, 'God has disclosed himself', and the muddy world swallows up any clear evidence. They say, 'Salvation has been achieved', and the place is littered with broken, incomplete people. They affirm 'Death is overcome', and another friend dies the day after.

And then again, there are all these other ways of seeing it interpreted by other faiths. Where do you start? It would take a lifetime to explore any properly, yet why should you take any other less seriously? You dismiss them before you understand them, and some of them are quite different. That seems extraordinary too, that the truth should be so fragmented, or that there should be so much error, whichever it is.

SNARL Well, why not drop it all, and get on with the things you do know and believe? You'll have no problem filling your days, and you won't go making rash and premature commitments to gospels you haven't even compared seriously with the others on the market.

SWITHER I can't. It unsettles me. Just imagine that the world
114

might be more truly known in terms of another condition it hasn't yet reached. What if we are being loved into our true existence, and only actually touch it on tiptoe at the odd moments when we find ourselves given absolute freedom to be. What if that freedom anticipates an unlimited possibility which can't be undermined by time or space or death or anything. Such a 'world' would be so strange that it makes me wonder if I know anything. Yet all that makes sense of me here and now *demands* that as its completeness. Anything less makes me absurd. But it seems so overwhelming a suggestion, and so hard to get at through the whole paraphernalia of creeds and churches and traditions that have struggled with it. But maybe that's what they've all been on about. And if struggling with it has any relation to making it possible, then you just have to do it, whatever deep end you find yourself at. That, at least, I believe. That possibility is worth battering at with all your resources.

can you choose

SNARL   Even if it never happens?

SWITHER   I think so. Even if it never happens.

SNARL   My God, you are a fool!

DISCUSSION QUESTIONS

Does it strike you as a good way to approach questions of belief to ask: 'What would be different if it were true/false?'

How do you think things would be different if, for instance, Christianity were true or false (instead of whichever you take it to be)?

Do you think that either disputant in the above dialogue could have offered better arguments on his own side?

FOR FURTHER READING

A. R. Vidler, ed., *Objections to Christian Belief*. Constable.
H. J. Blackham, ed., *Objections to Humanism*. Constable.
I. Ramsey, *On Being Sure in Religion*. Athlone Press.

INDEX